# JESUS AIN'T NO ROCK STAR!
## An exposé on the error of modern Christianity

By Rev. Josh W. Jones

JESUS AIN'T NO ROCK STAR!

Copyright © 2017 by Josh W. Jones

All rights reserved. In accordance with the U.S. Copyright Act of 1976, the scanning, uploading, and electronic sharing of any part of this book without the permission of the publisher is unlawful piracy and theft of the author's intellectual property. If you would like to use material from this book, prior written permission must be obtained by contacting the publisher. Thank you for your support of the author's rights.

Unless otherwise indicated, all scripture quotations are taken from the New King James Version of the Bible. Copyright © 1982 by Thomas Nelson, INC. Used by permission. All rights reserved

Cover Photo by Olaf Herschbach © 123RF.com

Inside the Gate Publishing
231 E. State Street
Jacksonville, IL 62650
www.insidethegate.org

# Contents

Foreword — 7

Introduction — 9

1. God's Word — 13

2. Hey Jesus, Can I Have Your Autograph? — 25

3. The Holy Who? — 37

4. The Hypocrite Church — 53

5. Making My Own way — 61

6. Multiple Roads — 71

7. We'll All Make Heaven — 79

8. Once Saved, Always Saved — 89

9. Grace! Let's Party! — 99

10. Lord Make Me Rich! — 111

11. God's a Jerk — 121

12. Salvation Experience — 133

Afterword — 139

References — 143

# Foreword

The book you're about to read has been in the works for decades, one might even say, for centuries. Of course I don't speak of my personal research or years of experience, that would be a mathematical impossibility. I'm referring to the twisting of the gospel that has taken place since its inception; leading to the culmination of the issues that plague the modern day church, which must be addressed in this hour.

As a minister, I experience and deal with the issues that these skewed doctrines have caused people on a daily basis. My intention in writing this book is not to attack or discredit anyone or any organization. The desire I have is to help people understand how the doctrine of many modern day churches is actually hindering their relationship with God, rather than increasing them in it.

The children of God must put aside their denominational differences and focus on the mission at hand, which is to reach the lost. The only way this can be done is to cut out the self serving doctrine that the church today has adopted, and get back to the true word of God. Think of this book as a reference work to guide you in spotting false doctrine by referencing you back to the Bible itself. In this book I will be speaking to nonbelievers that may pick this book up as well. My intent is for everyone to take something away from this, not just devout Christians.

As you may have already noticed, my writing style is unorthodox. I get to the point quickly and state it plainly, some may say crudely, with the intent that everyone who picks up this book will understand what is being said. I believe this is what God intended for us all to do, put aside our ego and speak his word clearly and simply. As the Apostle Paul wrote:

*"But I fear, lest somehow, as the serpent deceived Eve by his craftiness, so your minds may be corrupted from the simplicity that is in Christ. For if he who comes preaches another Jesus whom we have not preached, or if you receive a different spirit which you have not received, or a different gospel which you have not accepted—you may well put up with it!"*
*2 Corinthians 11:3-4*

I encourage you while reading this book to kick off your shoes, get comfortable, and follow me back to the grass roots of God's word. All the pomp of allure of modern day doctrine can't compare with the power and simplicity of the true word of God if you just choose to embrace it.

# Introduction

Within just a few years of Christ's death, the church had already begun to go astray. At the time, the apostles and others who had personally walked with Jesus and heard his teachings, were able to go quickly in most cases, and correct the error that was taking place within the early church. Or at least send word in the form of a letter to provide instruction and attempt to bring correction. The apostles knew false doctrine was one of the biggest threats to the church and to the individual believer as well. We see this cited in the book of Acts.

*"Therefore take heed to yourselves and to all the flock, among which the Holy Spirit has made you overseers, to shepherd the church of God which He purchased with His own blood. For I know this, that after my departure savage wolves will come in among you, not sparing the flock. Also from among yourselves men will rise up, speaking perverse things, to draw away the disciples after themselves." Acts 20:28-30*

Verse 30 sums up the purpose of the reason for the preaching of this false doctrine well, *"...to draw away the disciples after themselves."* False doctrine and false teachers are self seeking. The intent in most cases is not to deliberately lead people away from Jesus, but rather to glorify themselves. This is done by misconstruing, adding to, or taking away from scripture to make it more appealing to the listener. Paul brought this to Timothy's attention in saying,

*"For the time will come when they will not endure sound doctrine, but according to their own desires, because they have itching ears, they will heap up for themselves teachers; and they will turn their ears away from the truth, and be turned aside to fables." 2 Timothy 4:3-4*

What a picture of the modern day church. Many choose to hear what they want to hear and revolt against the preaching of the truth.

After the passing of the apostles the church continued to grow despite heavy persecution and resistance from the Roman Empire. That is, until Constantine converted to Christianity in the year A.D. 312 which soon after lead to the legalization of Christianity across the empire. Unfortunately, what would seemingly be a great victory for the Church; was also one of the biggest introductions of false doctrine into Christianity. Rather than fully embrace Christ and his teachings, the Romans exchanged one set of pagan rituals and deities for another. Though claiming to follow the teaching of Christ they created and worshipped saints, introduced many rituals, and glorified Jesus' mother Mary to a place of intercession that Christ alone holds.

*"For there is one God and one Mediator between God and men, the Man Christ Jesus" 1 Timothy 2:5*

This "new" form of Christianity, known as Roman Catholicism, was and is widely received and accepted. Sadly, false doctrine many times is accepted due to a lack of knowledge of the Word of God.

Within the teachings of Christ, there is no instruction to set up different denominations based on an individual's personal desires; just the opposite in fact.

*"With all lowliness and gentleness, with longsuffering, bearing with one another in love, endeavoring to keep the unity of the Spirit in the bond of peace. There is one body and one Spirit, just as you were called in one hope of your calling; one Lord, one faith, one baptism; one God and Father of all, who is above all, and through all, and in you all." Ephesians 4:2-6*

Nevertheless, with the birth of Catholicism came the first split in the Church. Many more splits were soon to follow throughout the ages, becoming what we now know as denominations.

Now here we are, nearly 2,000 years have gone by since Christ walked the Earth. He is still the most talked about and followed person in all of history. But what about the Church He founded? Has it followed the path in which He intended? The all around answer is no, in most cases it hardly resembles its intended state. As men often do, they've corrupted it. Instituting and continuing to institute regulations, procedures, and beliefs that have little to nothing to do with the teaching of Christ. Most estimates show that there are close to 40 different Christian denominations. Each with its own set of beliefs; spawned by the egotistical hearts of men. This division is detrimental to the work of Christ, and Jesus himself illustrated what happens with division.

*"If a kingdom is divided against itself, that kingdom cannot stand. And if a house is divided against itself, that house cannot stand." Mark 3:24-25*

It's time to reunite folks. The division, the infighting, and the drive for individual denominational gain have weakened Christianity enough. As the body of Christ we must put aside our differences and return to the original mission given to us by the Lord, which is leading people to Him and unto salvation.

*"And He said to them, "Go into all the world and preach the gospel to every creature. He who believes and is baptized will be saved; but he who does not believe will be condemned." Mark 16:15-16*

# Chapter 1: God's Word

Universally, the majority of people believe in God, 89% to be exact; according to the latest Gallup poll, taken in June of 2016.[1] While that seems encouraging, what about the percentage of people that believe the Bible is the literal word of God? That number is astoundingly low, only 24% in a May 2017 Gallup poll stated they believed in the entirety of the Bible.[2] That folks is a major problem.

*"For the word of the LORD is right, And all His work is done in truth." Psalm 33:4*

The Bible alone is our instruction from God, the backbone which supports our relationship with Him. Like the human body, if you remove the backbone, the body falls flat. In the same way, the rejection of God's word will cause your relationship with him, to fall flat.

From the beginning of creation, God wanted a close relationship with man; so much so that he came down and met with Adam and Eve in the Garden of Eden during the cool of the day.

*"And they heard the sound of the LORD God walking in the garden in the cool of the day, and Adam and his wife hid themselves from the presence of the LORD God among the trees of the garden." Genesis 3:8*

Sadly, due to the sin of Adam, God could no longer abide in the presence of man. The sin separation is what led to the need for the written word of God that he has given through the prophets and apostles. Without sin entering in, God would have continued to meet with man even as the population grew and He would have orally instructed the world in His ways.

In His love for us, He gave us the written Word to maintain communication and relationship with us. What an awesome thing to think about. When God could have written us off due to sin, and left us to fend for ourselves, He still desired relationship with us. Therefore, the denial of God's Word is blasphemous and who do we think we are to question Him?

*"What is man that You are mindful of him, And the son of man that You visit him?" Psalm 8:4*

## Is It Really God?

After establishing the need for the Word of God, the most common issue becomes whether or not the Bible is actually God breathed or just written by men from time past. The Word of God itself reveals the answer.

*"For we did not follow cunningly devised fables when we made known to you the power and coming of our Lord Jesus Christ, but were eyewitnesses of His majesty. For He received from God the Father honor and glory when such a voice came to Him from the Excellent Glory: **"This is My beloved Son, in whom I am well pleased."** And we heard this voice which came*

*from heaven when we were with Him on the holy mountain. And so we have the prophetic word confirmed, which you do well to heed as a light that shines in a dark place, until the day dawns and the morning star rises in your hearts; knowing this first, that no prophecy of Scripture is of any private interpretation, for prophecy never came by the will of man, but holy men of God spoke as they were moved by the Holy Spirit." 2 Peter 1:16-21*

Using reasonable logic, give this some thought. If the men that physically wrote the Bible, Peter in this instance, devised the text through their own mind and thought process; why would they attribute it to the inspiration of the Holy Spirit? It is not in the nature of human beings to attribute our own work to someone else, yet we see this throughout the entirety of the Bible. The revelation, the power, and the authority given to the men of the Bible was always attributed back to God and the Holy Spirit; who himself is God. If you're not familiar with the Holy Spirit, this may be slightly hard to grasp at this point; but will be clarified in chapter three. Just understand for now, that these men were not speaking of their own accord or through their own knowledge.

*"And my speech and my preaching were not with persuasive words of human wisdom, but in demonstration of the Spirit and of power, that your faith should not be in the wisdom of men but in the power of God." 1 Corinthians 2:4*

# Biblical Contradictions

Now, some of you may ask the question; "Why are there seemingly so many contradictions throughout the Bible?" The answer is a simple one, perspective. As any good detective will tell you, details of eye witness testimony always differ slightly; while the centrality of the event remains the same. When every detail from multiple witnesses matches exactly, that typically means the story was rehearsed. So discrepancies from one eye witness account to another in the Bible actually give credit to its legitimacy.

Look at this example for instance. Four people see a young blonde female run over by a vehicle. Two people say the driver is a white male; two people say the driver is a black female. Three say the vehicle is a brown SUV, while the fourth says a dark grey sedan. Though each account differs on what most would say are major details, the story remains the same; a young blonde female was hit by a vehicle. This is a prime example of how the Bible was written, from different perspectives, with one main story throughout; which is the need for a Savior. That Savior of course, was and is Jesus Christ.

*"For God so loved the world that He gave His only begotten Son, that whoever believes in Him should not perish but have everlasting life. For God did not send His Son into the world to condemn the world, but that the world through Him might be saved." John 3:16-17*

Most likely, if you are an opponent of the Bible based on the fact that you say it is written by men and it contradicts itself, you are now thinking I just contradicted myself by saying the writers had different perspective. Because if the writers used their own perspective to write, then the Bible is not inspired and authored by God's Spirit but rather men. And you would be right if the Holy Spirit, when speaking through us, took over our minds and controlled us like a robot telling us what to say. But that would be a misinterpretation of the way that the Holy Spirit operates.

The Holy Spirit guides you rather than controls you. In guiding the writers of the Bible, the Holy Spirit impressed upon them what to include, not what was to be said when memorializing events that the writer themselves experienced. An example of this would be John, witnessing the crucifixion of Jesus.

*"So when Jesus had received the sour wine, He said, **"It is finished!"** And bowing His head, He gave up His spirit." John 19:30*

In John's account here, the Holy Spirit did not tell John to write that Jesus said **"It is finished!"** but for John to simply record what he personally heard and witnessed. This makes it not only plausible, but rational to believe that others who witnessed the crucifixion may record a slightly different account. This is due to the Holy Spirit leading them to write what THEY saw and heard. However, in the end, all accounts are rooted in the same truth that Jesus Christ died on the cross.

## A Cruel and Barbaric God

Beyond the aforementioned, one of the biggest stumbling blocks to any person that picks up the Bible, is how to comprehend how a loving God could seemingly be so cruel and the tales so barbaric. After all, in the Bible you see the Earth being flooded,

*"So He destroyed all living things which were on the face of the ground: both man and cattle, creeping thing and bird of the air. They were destroyed from the earth. Only Noah and those who were with him in the ark remained alive. And the waters prevailed on the earth one hundred and fifty days. Genesis 7:23-24*

Cities being destroyed,

*"Then the LORD rained brimstone and fire on Sodom and Gomorrah, from the LORD out of the heavens. So He overthrew those cities, all the plain, all the inhabitants of the cities, and what grew on the ground." Genesis 19:24-25*

And a man impaled in the head with a tent peg.

*"Then Jael, Heber's wife, took a tent peg and took a hammer in her hand, and went softly to him and drove the peg into his temple, and it went down into the ground; for he was fast asleep and weary. So he died." Judges 4:21*

The first step in reconciling this dilemma is to understand that the Old Testament must be separated from the New Testament. The law of the Old Covenant brought judgment and death due to the inability of man to keep the law. Without the perfect sacrifice of Christ, sins could not be completely forgiven, only pushed back. The grace of the New Covenant brought life through salvation due to the perfect sacrifice of Jesus Christ. This allows us to be judged based on Christ's perfect life, rather than our own sinful actions. This makes us free from the wrath of God and His judgment seen in the Old Testament. That is, if one has accepted Christ as their savior.

The second step is to come to the realization that God is just in all His actions. He does not act on impulse nor does He desire to see His children perish. But due to His righteousness, He must take action on those who do evil.

*"Behold, God is mighty, but despises no one; He is mighty in strength of understanding. He does not preserve the life of the wicked, But gives justice to the oppressed. Job 36:5-6*

In each of the three examples previously given, there was a just cause behind the action; number one, the flood.

*"Then the LORD saw that the wickedness of man was great in the earth, and that every intent of the thoughts of his heart was only evil continually. And the LORD was sorry that He had made man on the earth, and He was grieved in His heart. So the LORD said,* **"I will destroy man whom I have created from the face of the earth, both man and beast, creeping thing and birds of the air, for I am sorry that I have made them."** *But Noah found grace in the eyes of the LORD." Genesis 6:5-8*

We see here that God did not simply decide to destroy all of creation because He felt like it, but He had to due to the wickedness of man. Yet even in God's disappointment and judgment, He looked to extend grace to anyone that would seek Him; which He did for Noah and his family.

Let's look at number two, the destruction of Sodom and Gomorrah.

*"Look, this was the iniquity of your sister Sodom: She and her daughter had pride, fullness of food, and abundance of idleness; neither did she strengthen the hand of the poor and needy. And they were haughty and committed abomination before Me; therefore I took them away as I saw fit." Ezekiel 16:49-50*

Beyond their pride and their greed, sexual immorality ran rampant to an extent modern civilization can hardly fathom. They even tried to rape the angels sent by the Lord.

*"Now before they lay down, the men of the city, the men of Sodom, both old and young, all the people from every quarter, surrounded the house. And they called to Lot and said to him, "Where are the men who came to you tonight? Bring them out to us that we may know them carnally." Genesis 19:4-5*

Again, even with the depravity of these cities, God looks to extend grace to anyone who would look to Him.

*"Far be it from You to do such a thing as this, to slay the righteous with the wicked, so that the righteous should be as the wicked; far be it from You! Shall not the Judge of all the earth do right?" So the LORD said,*

***"If I find in Sodom fifty righteous within the city, then I will spare all the place for their sakes."*** *Genesis 18:25-26*

And of course, God goes on to tell Abraham that if he finds even ten righteous in the entire city, he will spare it. However, ten righteous men could not be found in the entirety of the population, thus leading to its destruction.

While that sheds light on God's judgment, what about the barbaric actions of the third example given? That issue simply comes down to understanding the culture and what was going on in the world at that point in history. During this time there was a state of anarchy, the Israelites did whatever they wanted and turned away from God time and again.

*"Then the children of Israel did evil in the sight of the LORD, and served the Baals." Judges 2:11*

*"In those days there was no king in Israel; everyone did what was right in his own eyes." Judges 21:25*

With the absence of God in the lives of the Israelites, they suffered many defeats and much misery. Not because God was punishing them, but because they chose not to serve God which allowed evil in. The same still happens today, when people or a nation walk away from God, chaos and tragedy are sure to follow. And when the misery becomes more than the people can bear, they cry out to God. This is exactly what the Israelites did time and again, and God hearing their cries, would extend His grace by providing them a judge to deliver them.

The judge in the particular story that we are looking at is Deborah, she was brought to power by God and He used her to deliver Israel from the Canaanites. She appointed Barak to lead Israel's army against the army of King Jabin, which was commanded by Sisera. By the end of the battle not one of Sisera's men were left standing, but Sisera managed to escape. Barak pursued, and Sisera took refuge in the tent of Jael; where he thought he would be safe. This of course is where Jael drove the tent peg into Sisera's head.

Whether or not the Lord moved upon her to do such a barbaric thing, one can only speculate. What we do know is this was a time of war, and the people had walked away from God and did what each saw fit; which led to the atrocities found in the Old Testament. These stories are there, not to scare people into following God, but rather to remind the reader what happens when we forsake God to follow our own desires. Attempting to judge God as barbaric or cruel based on the poor decisions of men is like trying to blame ice cream for making someone obese, it's nonsensical.

## I Don't Believe It All

"Well, say what you will, but I only believe the words in red that Jesus said." If pastors had a dollar for every time they heard that one, the church wouldn't need to take offering. To dismiss any part of the Bible is to dismiss the whole thing.

*"All Scripture is given by inspiration of God, and is profitable for doctrine, for reproof, for correction, for instruction in righteousness, that the man of God may*

*be complete, thoroughly equipped for every good work." 2 Timothy 3:16-17*

Think back to a time in math class when you were first being introduced to word problems. There always came a time when you got to a question that did not have enough information to solve. This of course is called a trick question. But think of how you felt as a child, not knowing if there really wasn't enough information to solve it or if you just weren't quite smart enough to figure it out. It's a pretty helpless and frustrating feeling.

That insolvable, not enough information question is exactly what life is when only portions of the Bible are taken for truth. A feeling of hopelessness, helplessness, and confusion rule the mind. This eventually leads many to walk away from God, feeling as though he doesn't have the answer, when the answer is there all along if one takes the entirety of the scripture to heart.

*"This Book of the Law shall not depart from your mouth, but you shall meditate in it day and night, that you may observe to do according to all that is written in it. For then you will make your way prosperous, and then you will have good success." Joshua 1:8*

## Think About It

Excuses to try and delegitimize the Word of God are merely feeble attempts to excuse one's ungodly lifestyle. The sinful nature of man is to justify our actions and dictate right from wrong. But what is right and wrong without the Word of God? If each person is left to judge what is good or bad based on their own personal opinions, then there is no plumb line with which to measure to; therefore making all things permissible. One cannot even say that their benchmark of right and wrong is the law of the land without validating God. Many laws against capital crimes were originally instituted based on the Word of God, whether the writer's of the law were aware of it or not. Most people universally believe it is wrong to kill, steal, cheat, and lie; which is based on God's law. So why is it so hard to accept the other instruction God has given us? Bottom line is; we must get back to embracing God's entire word as literal for the betterment of the country and world.

# Chapter 2:
## Hey Jesus, Can I Have Your Autograph?

Jesus Christ, the Lord and Savior of the entire human race, was prophesied about and anticipated for thousands of years. He opened blind eyes.

*"So Jesus answered and said to him, **"What do you want Me to do for you?"** The blind man said to Him, "Rabboni, that I may receive my sight." Then Jesus said to him, **"Go your way; your faith has made you well."** And immediately he received his sight and followed Jesus on the road." Mark 10:51-52*

He healed the sick.

*"And Jesus went about all Galilee, teaching in their synagogues, preaching the gospel of the kingdom, and healing all kinds of sickness and all kinds of disease among the people. Then His fame went throughout all Syria; and they brought to Him all sick people who were afflicted with various diseases and torments, and those who were demon-possessed, epileptics, and paralytics; and He healed them." Matthew 4:23-24*

And He raised the dead.

*"Jesus said to her, **"Did I not say to you that if you would believe you would see the glory of God?"** Then they took away the stone from the place where the dead man was lying. And Jesus lifted up His eyes and*

*said, **"Father, I thank You that You have heard Me. And I know that You always hear Me, but because of the people who are standing by I said this, that they may believe that You sent Me."** Now when He had said these things, He cried with a loud voice, **"Lazarus, come forth!"** And he who had died came out bound hand and foot with grave clothes, and his face was wrapped with a cloth. Jesus said to them, **"Loose him, and let him go."** John 11:40-44*

Yet much of the world today treats Jesus as though He's nothing more than a rock star, here to entertain and please us. Look around at modern society and how it engages the Son of God. Jesus bumper stickers, t-shirts, and bobble heads. Not to mention the way His name is tossed around flippantly as an expletive. How far this world has slipped from the reverence it once paid to our Lord.

*"The next day a great multitude that had come to the feast, when they heard that Jesus was coming to Jerusalem, took branches of palm trees and went out to meet Him, and cried out: "Hosanna! 'Blessed is He who comes in the name of the LORD!' The King of Israel!" John 12:13*

## Jesus Paraphernalia

Some of you may be thinking that I'm a legalistic, super spiritual weirdo, against anything modern. That would be an incorrect assumption. You see there is nothing wrong with a Jesus shirt or bumper sticker as long as it's not sacrilegious. Things like that can actually be a great ice breaker for a conversation about the Lord with a stranger. The issue with any product depicting Jesus lies with the spirit in which it is used. Every action has a spirit behind it, whether it is good, bad, honest, dishonest, etc. If one chooses to buy products that depict the Lord, they should only be doing so with the intent to bring glory to Him.

However, many times this is not the case. People use Jesus as a shtick. Poking fun at the crucifixion, resurrection, and salvation associated with Him. Jesus Christ is not a party favor or a punch line. Christians must be responsible with the way in which we depict our faith through the use of products pertaining to God and our Lord. It is also the responsibility of the believer to stand up for Christ in a manner consistent with the Bible; if you see someone portraying Jesus as a joke. Defending Christ is not only your chance to witness to people, but it's what we are expected to do. To not defend Christ as a believer is the same as denying him.

*"Therefore whoever confesses Me before men, him I will also confess before My Father who is in heaven. But whoever denies Me before men, him I will also deny before My Father who is in heaven."*
*Matthew 10:32-33*

# God and Man

Along with the misuse of Jesus products goes the misuse of His name. Many people use the name of Jesus Christ with the frequency of any other slang. We have all heard someone yell "Jesus Christ" when something unexpected or bad happens. I'll be honest; I've done it in the past. Most likely you have too, or maybe you still do. It can be somewhat understandable when a person who doesn't know Christ uses His name in that way, they don't know better. The sad fact is, just as many self professed Christians are using it in the same way!

The odd thing with the majority of Christians who use the name of Jesus as slang, do their best to keep the commandment of not taking the Lord's name in vain.

*"You shall not take the name of the LORD your God in vain, for the LORD will not hold him guiltless who takes His name in vain." Exodus 20:7*

There could not be a better example of an oxymoron than one who attempts to refrain from using "God" out of context to prevent taking His name in vain. Yet uses "Jesus" as slang freely, because Jesus is God!

*"In the beginning was the Word, and the Word was with God, and the Word was God." John 1:1*

*"And the Word became flesh and dwelt among us, and we beheld His glory, the glory as of the only begotten of the Father, full of grace and truth." John 1:14*

The Lord Jesus was 100% God and 100% man. He had to be man to be tested and live as we do in order to redeem us. But one must never forget that He is also God. Using the name of Jesus in any context outside of prayer or worship, is taking the Lord's name in vain. Christians must set an example more so today than ever. If we expect to win people for the Lord we must watch our words and actions carefully so we don't ruin our witness. By this, I mean to appear as a hypocrite by claiming to be Christian but acting like the world.

# Power in His Name

The name of Jesus is more than just punctuation at the end of a prayer. In His name there is power unlike that found anywhere else on Earth. The Lord gave us the use of His name to work miracles on Earth just as He did, but with even greater power. What an amazing gift!

*"Most assuredly, I say to you, he who believes in Me, the works that I do he will do also; and greater works than these he will do, because I go to My Father. And whatever you ask in My name, that I will do, that the Father may be glorified in the Son. If you ask anything in My name, I will do it." John 14:12-14*

Notice Jesus qualifies His statement by saying **"he who believes in Me"** will do these things. The power of Christ is open only to those who believe and follow Him. This is a commonly overlooked caveat by many who attempt to evoke the power of Christ without having a relationship with Him. Then after their attempt to use the power of Jesus name falls flat, they blame Him as if He did something wrong.

In very few occasions the Lord will work through someone using the name of Jesus that doesn't have a relationship with Him. He will only do so if He knows that it will bring that person into relationship with Him. This however, is not a common occurrence as miracles typically don't bring about salvation; due to the stubbornness of man. The takeaway is, in most cases without having a relationship with Christ, the command "In Jesus name" will fall flat. It can even be dangerous.

*"Then some of the itinerant Jewish exorcists took it upon themselves to call the name of the Lord Jesus over those who had evil spirits, saying, "We exorcise you by the Jesus whom Paul preaches." Also there were seven sons of Sceva, a Jewish chief priest, who did so. And the evil spirit answered and said, "Jesus I know, and Paul I know; but who are you?" Then the man in whom the evil spirit was leaped on them, overpowered them, and prevailed against them, so that they fled out of that house naked and wounded. This became known both to all Jews and Greeks dwelling in Ephesus; and fear fell on them all, and the name of the Lord Jesus was magnified." Acts 19:13-17*

When the name of Jesus is used correctly by those that follow and have a relationship with Him, the result will be miraculous if that person's faith rests solely in the Lord.

*"Now Peter and John went up together to the temple at the hour of prayer, the ninth hour. And a certain man lame from his mother's womb was carried, whom they laid daily at the gate of the temple which is called Beautiful, to ask alms from those who entered the temple; who, seeing Peter and John about to go into the temple, asked for alms. And fixing his eyes on him, with John, Peter said, "Look at us." So he gave them his attention, expecting to receive something from*

*them. Then Peter said, "Silver and gold I do not have, but what I do have I give you: In the name of Jesus Christ of Nazareth, rise up and walk." And he took him by the right hand and lifted him up, and immediately his feet and ankle bones received strength." Acts 3:1-7*

Sadly, many today teach that the power of Jesus was for the twelve apostles only. That could not be further from the truth and is keeping the modern Church from functioning in the way that it was intended. Simply look at what Jesus said when the apostles brought it to His attention, that someone was evoking His name that was not an apostle.

*"Now John answered and said, "Master, we saw someone casting out demons in Your name, and we forbade him because he does not follow with us." But Jesus said to him,* ***Do not forbid him, for he who is not against us is on our side." Luke 9:49-50***

If Jesus did not intend for anyone other than the apostles to perform miracles and exercise power in His name, He would have addressed it there in the scripture. People often wonder why we, the modern Church, don't see miracles like we see in the Bible. It's because most of the Church stopped believing in them! After centuries of preachers that don't know their ear from their elbow taught against the miracle working power of Jesus, people became accustomed to not seeing or operating in it.

The Church needs to engage the power of Jesus. He ordained it for us because He knew the things that we would face in this world. He knew that without that power, the Church would not succeed. Knowing people would come against it, saying Jesus was just a man and would turn away from the faith. Since the Church has begun to cease operating in the power of Jesus, man has done exactly that; turned away.

Look at the statistics for yourself of the drastic decline of Christianity. It's not because the Lord has walked away or lost His power, He is still the same. It's us that have changed; we've given up the power and lost the zeal. We must get back to operating in Christ the way He intended, exuding His power for the betterment of His Church, that we may reach the lost!

*"Jesus Christ is the same yesterday, today, and forever." Hebrews 13:8*

# Our Friend Jesus

In this world of hurt, people often seek comfort in others; whether it is in friends, family, or a spouse. The problem with that is; people will fail you. But the Lord Jesus Christ will never fail you. His love is endless, He is always there to answer when you call, and He will meet all of your needs in ways that no human being ever could. He longs for us to come to Him and desires that we be a friend to Him. And He will be a friend to us if we simply do what is required of us.

*"You are My friends if you do whatever I command you. No longer do I call you servants, for a servant does not know what his master is doing; but I have*

*called you friends, for all things that I heard from My Father I have made known to you." John 15:14-15*

There are some of you out there saying, "I don't want a friendship with anyone that requires something of me." If that's the case you will never have a true friend, at least not for very long. Every friendship and relationship has basic requirements, unspoken rules if you will. Any person you plan on having a meaningful relationship with expects honesty, communication, and respect. The vast majority of people understands these basic rules of friendship, and implements them to the best of their ability with those they care about. So why do so many not have the same attitude towards their savior Jesus Christ?

You know the attitude I'm talking about, the people that are in church when life is tough, but nowhere around when things are going well for them. Or the people that ask for prayer on social media when they are going through something traumatic, but once trouble has passed them by, they resume advocating that prayer and the Ten Commandments don't belong in public places.

Jesus Christ is not at our every whim, there to be called upon only when we need Him. While He is faithful and longsuffering, don't expect to live a blessed life during the seasons in which you're not walking with Him. If you do not do your part to maintain the relationship, you will miss out on the good things God has planned for you.

# Think About It

Christ does not want a part time relationship with you. His desire is for His Spirit to dwell within you, to have constant communication with you, and to be so deeply engrained in you that you exude Him at all times.

*"I have been crucified with Christ; it is no longer I who live, but Christ lives in me; and the life which I now live in the flesh I live by faith in the Son of God, who loved me and gave Himself for me." Galatians 2:20*

This complete release of yourself and the giving of your heart to the Lord is what water baptism symbolizes. And while we're on the subject, understand that the water does not save your soul. Rather, it is an outward sign of the inward change that has taken place. This is why baptism is to be complete submersion under water, rather than a sprinkling on the head. Otherwise, the symbolism is Christ having only part of you. Again, baptism is symbolism of a heart change, not a salvation experience. With this comes the understanding that since the salvation does not come from the baptism itself, but from belief in ones heart, baptizing a baby does not save their soul.

*"That if you confess with your mouth the Lord Jesus and believe in your heart that God has raised Him from the dead, you will be saved." Romans 10:9*

An infant cannot decide to accept Jesus in their hearts, nor can they comprehend it, therefore they do not need to be baptized. One may dedicate their baby before the

Lord, but this is a pledge for the parents to raise their child in the way of the Lord. Through God's grace a child is accepted into Heaven without formally accepting Christ until they reach the age of accountability, knowing right from wrong.

*"For the unbelieving husband is sanctified by the wife, and the unbelieving wife is sanctified by the husband; otherwise your children would be unclean, but now they are holy." 1 Corinthians 7:14*

Give yourself fully to Christ. Allow Him to work in your life and meet your needs. He has your best interests at heart and you will never have a better friend than Him. Use the power which He has given to those who believe in Him that the Church may return to its former glory. He will give you as much of Himself as you want, all you have to do is ask!

# Notes

# Chapter 3:
# The Holy Who?

Here we go. Let's discuss the most highly debated member of the trinity. The reason for the Holy Spirit being so highly debated is anyone's guess, but the most reasonable thing would seem to be the lack of understanding of Him. Before even approaching His function, let's address the elephant in the room; those who even doubt His existence. Considering that Jesus Himself referenced the Holy Spirit numerous times.

*"Go therefore and make disciples of all the nations, baptizing them in the name of the Father and of the Son and of the Holy Spirit." Matthew 28:19*

*"If you love Me, keep My commandments. And I will pray the Father, and He will give you another Helper, that He may abide with you forever— the Spirit of truth, whom the world cannot receive, because it neither sees Him nor knows Him; but you know Him, for He dwells with you and will be in you." John 14:15-17*

Debating the existence of the Holy Spirit is to doubt the Word of God. We already discussed this in chapter one, if you skipped over it, please go back and read it; because this chapter is going to discuss how the Holy Spirit functions.

Many people rarely, if ever, hear the Holy Spirit mentioned outside of prayer. Accurate teaching on the operation of the Holy Spirit is almost nonexistent in the modern Church. Without solid foundational teaching, how is one to understand the role He plays in the life of the believer and nonbeliever alike?

## Holy Spirit and the Nonbeliever

In the life of the nonbeliever, meaning one who does not follow Christ, the Holy Spirit has one major function. That function is to draw that person to Jesus Christ with the goal of them accepting Him as their savior. The Holy Spirit does this in two ways.

The first way is attempting to keep the nonbeliever out of harm's way by speaking to them, so that they may reach a place of salvation. The way in which He speaks is soft, most nonbelievers refer to it as their conscience or their instinct; that thing that a person feels within themselves, urging them not do a certain thing or go a certain place. Of course a person has the free will to choose to heed the warning or dismiss it.

The second way the Holy Spirit works is to lead a nonbeliever into a situation that presents Christ to them. He may do this by putting the person with a believer during a high stress situation. Or the person may suddenly feel a desire to go to church, read the Bible, or call on a Christian friend. If the individual never chooses to accept Christ, this is as far the work of the Holy Spirit can go. The Holy Spirit always works directly in line with the will of God and through the direction of Jesus Christ.

*"However, when He, the Spirit of truth, has come, He will guide you into all truth; for He will not speak on His own authority, but whatever He hears He will speak; and He will tell you things to come. He will glorify Me, for He will take of what is Mine and declare it to you." John 16:13-14*

## Holy Spirit and the Believer

The work of the Holy Spirit in the life of a believer is much more extensive. Of course if one is a believer, the Holy Spirit has already performed the function previously stated in the explanation of His work on a nonbeliever. But when the individual accepts Christ, the Holy Spirit can then reside within that person. This is the indwelling of the Holy Spirit. It is important to note here what the description of a believer is; one who has accepted Christ. As stated in chapter one, many people believe in the Lord, but refuse to receive Him.

*"There is therefore now no condemnation to those who are in Christ Jesus, who do not walk according to the flesh, but according to the Spirit." Romans 8:1*

*"But you are not in the flesh but in the Spirit, if indeed the Spirit of God dwells in you. Now if anyone does not have the Spirit of Christ, he is not His." Romans 8:9*

The indwelling of the Holy Spirit comes automatically and immediately upon one accepting Christ as their Lord and savior. However, the infilling or baptism of the Holy Spirit is a separate and distinct event. The two things can happen simultaneously at salvation, but typically comes later as a believer grows with the Lord and asks to be baptized with the Holy Spirit.

The baptism with the Holy Spirit gives the believer unlimited power to operate in the gifts of the Spirit, given as the Lord sees fit. Super hero powers in the movies pale in comparison the real world power of the Holy Spirit. Of course I'm being humorous here, but I do so to make a point. Many people watch these movies and have the thought, even if only for a second, "I wish I had a super power." When the truth is a person can have supernatural powers if they will just give their hearts to Christ and ask Him to be baptized in the Holy Spirit. Yet somehow that seems farfetched while x-ray vision doesn't!

It is important to note the baptism and infilling with the Holy Spirit will always be accompanied with the initial evidence of speaking in other tongues.

*"When the Day of Pentecost had fully come, they were all with one accord in one place. And suddenly there came a sound from heaven, as of a rushing mighty wind, and it filled the whole house where they were sitting. Then there appeared to them divided tongues, as of fire, and one sat upon each of them. And they were all filled with the Holy Spirit and began to speak with other tongues, as the Spirit gave them utterance."*
*Acts 2:1-4*

*"While Peter was still speaking these words, the Holy Spirit fell upon all those who heard the word. And those of the circumcision who believed were astonished, as*

*many as came with Peter, because the gift of the Holy Spirit had been poured out on the Gentiles also. For they heard them speak with tongues and magnify God." Acts 10:44-46*

*"And it happened, while Apollos was at Corinth, that Paul, having passed through the upper regions, came to Ephesus. And finding some disciples he said to them, "Did you receive the Holy Spirit when you believed?" So they said to him, "We have not so much as heard whether there is a Holy Spirit." And he said to them, "Into what then were you baptized?" So they said, "Into John's baptism." Then Paul said, "John indeed baptized with a baptism of repentance, saying to the people that they should believe on Him who would come after him, that is, on Christ Jesus." When they heard this, they were baptized in the name of the Lord Jesus. And when Paul had laid hands on them, the Holy Spirit came upon them, and they spoke with tongues and prophesied." Acts 19:1-6*

## Gifts of the Spirit

As previously mentioned, with the baptism of the Holy Spirit, comes access to the gifts of the Spirit. There are nine gifts of the Spirit. A believer that is baptized in the Spirit may have one or more of the gifts; few may even have all of the gifts. The important thing to remember is that the gifts are given to edify the Church. They are not given to glorify the believer, and raise them above anyone else that they may boast.

*But the manifestation of the Spirit is given to each one for the profit of all: for to one is given the word of wisdom through the Spirit, to another the word of knowledge through the same Spirit, to another faith by the same Spirit, to another gifts of healings by the same Spirit, to another the working of miracles, to another prophecy, to another discerning of spirits, to another different kinds of tongues, to another the interpretation of tongues. But one and the same Spirit works all these things, distributing to each one individually as He wills. 1 Corinthians 12:7-11*

## Wisdom

The word of wisdom is insight into a situation that is placed in front of the believer whom the gift is operating through. The one operating in this gift will speak something given to them directly from God, which they in no way could have known naturally. The message of wisdom may be used to instruct an individual or a group of people in the plan the Lord has for them. This wisdom is temporary for the specific occasion and usually refers to future events; it is not a permanent state of divine genius.

## Knowledge

In modern society, the term wisdom and knowledge are almost interchangeable. When it comes to the gifts of the Spirit however, they are quite noticeably different. The gift of knowledge is a partial revelation of God's plan. This plan can relate to an individual, group of people, or an entire nation. A common place to see this gift in action is during an altar call at a church service. The minister displaying the gift may say something like

"Someone here has a heart condition that God is going to heal tonight." Notice the partial revelation, God does not give the name of the person or what the exact condition is; though He certainly could if He chose to. This gives the person whom the message is for, the option to choose to receive what God has for them or deny it. He will never force Himself on a person.

## Faith

Every person in the world that has the ability to think and function has faith. This is natural faith. It is the feeling one has that the car will start when they turn the key, or that their paycheck will be ready after working a certain amount of hours. Supernatural faith is believing in things we cannot see, but knowing beyond a shadow of a doubt it exists. This is the faith that brings us to salvation, by us believing in Jesus Christ.

The gift of faith is one that takes us through the toughest of times with confidence and assurance. It can also be used to ensure others who doubt, that things are going to be fine. The apostle Paul is a great example of this; he heard from the Lord and believed, displaying the gift of knowledge and faith. We too, like the apostle Paul, can hear from the Lord, every single day; if we pick up the Bible and read His message to us.

*"For there stood by me this night an angel of the God to whom I belong and whom I serve, saying, 'Do not be afraid, Paul; you must be brought before Caesar; and indeed God has granted you all those who sail with you.' Therefore take heart, men, for I believe God that it will be just as it was told me." Acts 27:23-25*

## Healings

No, that's not a typo. Look back at the scripture and you'll see that it says "gifts of healings" in the plural. The reason for this is because there are many different forms of healing. Some may need physical healing while another needs emotional or spiritual healing. This is the only gift that does operate through one human being to another. The gift of healing comes directly from Christ to the person needing to be healed. While the Holy Spirit may move upon someone to lay hands on the sick and pray for healing, the healing itself does not come from the person praying. This can be difficult for some to grasp, as the Lord may use the same individual in prayer for healing repeatedly. Leading many to believe that the individual is the one who holds the healing, this is not the case!

## Miracles

The working of miracles is a gift intended to display God's power and authority. A miracle defies all human logic and even the laws of science. There are a multitude of miracles in the Bible, from the parting of the Red Sea to the feeding of the 5,000, and water coming from a rock in the desert. The Holy Spirit gives this gift to defeat evil, give provision during times of desperate need, or free one from a life threatening circumstance.

## Prophecy

The gift of prophecy is speaking directly on the behalf of God. This may be to strengthen the Church, bring correction, or instruct the people what the Lord wants done. Prophecy will always be in line with the Bible and should be tested against the scripture. God will not and does not contradict Himself. Any prophecy brought forth that is contrary to anything written in the Bible, is not from God. Having the gift of prophecy does not necessarily mean that one is called to be a prophet.

## Discernment

Discerning or distinguishing between spirits is a valuable, but often low key gift. The gift of discernment is almost always used more frequently than any other gift in the life of a believer, or at least it should be. This gift helps the believer to judge human spirits, evil spirits, and the Holy Spirit. In the world of technology we live in today, there's access to a multitude of preachers on the internet and television. The gift of discernment will help one to sense false teaching before they fall prey to it. It is less talked about than many of the other gifts because it is not typically used to the knowledge of anyone else, whereas the other gifts can be seen or heard; though it can be used to call out an impure spirit as Jesus did to Peter.

*"But He [Jesus] turned and said to Peter,* ***"Get behind Me, Satan! You are an offense to Me, for you are not mindful of the things of God, but the things of men."*** *Matthew 16:23*

When a person is operating in the gift of discernment, they often get a feeling of discomfort as they sense the presence of someone with evil or impure intentions. It must be noted, that a person gifted with discernment, can only discern as much of God's will as they know.

And of course we come to know God's will more and more as we spend time studying the Bible.

Again the Holy Spirit can partially bestow this gift briefly on someone that is not baptized in the Spirit for personal protection or protection of the innocent. For instance, when a murder is apprehended by police and a reporter interviews those who have been in close proximity to the murderer, you'll often hear the same thing. "I had a bad gut feeling about him." This feeling is partial discernment working even in the unbeliever as a warning from the Holy Spirit. While others that barely knew the person and are not baptized in the spirit say, "Seemed like a nice guy to me, I can't believe it." They were not in a position of danger, nor were they operating in the gift of discernment, therefore lacked the ability to judge the spirit of the individual.

### Tongues and Interpretation

The gift of tongues and the interpretation of tongues go hand in hand. They are used in conjunction with one another to edify the Church. The gift of tongues is different than the tongues one receives at the baptism of the Holy Spirit. The tongues one receives and operates in after they are baptized in the Spirit is a personal prayer language, this is the Spirit which resides within you communicating directly with the Lord. This personal prayer language cannot be interpreted or understood by Satan or demon spirits.

*"For he who speaks in a tongue does not speak to men but to God, for no one understands him; however, in the spirit he speaks mysteries." 1 Corinthians 14:2*

The gift of tongues is a message directly from the Lord to the Church for the enhancement of worship in that particular service. It is up to the believer to yield to the Holy Spirit and deliver the message at the appropriate time during the service. He does not force one to speak!

The interpretation of tongues must follow a message in tongues in a church service. This allows the congregation to understand what the Lord is saying to them. Otherwise it will bring about confusion and disorder.

Speaking of disorder, it is extremely important for a church that the members do not to get caught up operating in the flesh rather than the Spirit. What I mean by that is if the same people week after week and month after month prophesy, fall out (pass out) in the Spirit, or run the aisles; they are not actually operating in the Spirit. That is a person imitating the Spirit to draw attention to themselves. Correction should be brought by the pastor or deacons in such a situation. While those actions mentioned above are things that may happen to a person that the Spirit has fallen on in a service, they won't take place every single service. The reason behind that is simple, though God is the same yesterday, today, and forever; He operates differently from one situation to the next in carrying out His will.

*"If anyone speaks in a tongue, let there be two or at the most three, each in turn, and let one interpret. But if there is no interpreter, let him keep silent in church, and let him speak to himself and to God."*
*1 Corinthians 14:27-28*

# Walking in the Spirit

When we have the Holy Spirit within us, we set aside sinful addictions and refrain from certain actions. This allows Christ to shine through in our life and our behavior. It does not mean one will ever reach perfection or that they are better than anyone else. It simply means they exude Christ more and more through their actions as the Holy Spirit works in their life. The scripture speaks clearly for itself.

*I say then: Walk in the Spirit, and you shall not fulfill the lust of the flesh. For the flesh lusts against the Spirit, and the Spirit against the flesh; and these are contrary to one another, so that you do not do the things that you wish. But if you are led by the Spirit, you are not under the law. Now the works of the flesh are evident, which are: adultery, fornication, uncleanness, lewdness, idolatry, sorcery, hatred, contentions, jealousies, outbursts of wrath, selfish ambitions, dissensions, heresies, envy, murders, drunkenness, revelries, and the like; of which I tell you beforehand, just as I also told you in time past, <u>that those who practice such things will not inherit the kingdom of God</u>." Galatians 5:16-21*

That last verse here is a powerful one. It shows that fulfilling our own desires leads to separation from God. In contrast, look at the work of the Spirit.

*"But the fruit of the Spirit is love, joy, peace, longsuffering, kindness, goodness, faithfulness, gentleness, self-control. Against such there is no law.*

*And those who are Christ's have crucified the flesh with its passions and desires. If we live in the Spirit, let us also walk in the Spirit." Galatians 5:22-25*

Notice the work of the flesh is double that of the fruit of the Spirit. Satan has devised so many sinful lusts for human beings to engage in, it is impossible without the help of the Holy Spirit to avoid them all. As the scripture states, the work of the flesh is obvious. That is why when we operate in the fruit of the Spirit we bring attention to Christ, because it is completely opposite of human nature.

## Is It for Me and Is It Necessary?

Many preachers will tell you that the Holy Spirit was only for the apostles. Some will say it was for the apostles and those who worked closely with them, only used to help spread the Gospel quickly to establish the early Church. Both those teachings are completely false and are in direct contradiction to the scripture.

*"And it shall come to pass in the last days, says God, That I will pour out of My Spirit on all flesh; Your sons and your daughters shall prophesy, Your young men shall see visions, Your old men shall dream dreams." Acts 2:17*

*"Then Peter said to them, "Repent, and let every one of you be baptized in the name of Jesus Christ for the remission of sins; and you shall receive the gift of the Holy Spirit. For the promise is to you and to your*

*children, and to all who are afar off, as many as the Lord our God will call." Acts 2:38-39*

Another issue the modern Church has with the Holy Spirit is whether or not the individual really needs Him. The answer to that is yes and no, depending on the context. Some try and profess that one must be baptized in the Holy Spirit to be saved and make it to Heaven. Not only is there no scripture to back that up, it's actually contrary to scripture.

*"Whoever calls on the name of the LORD shall be saved." Romans 10:13*

So clearly the answer to the question "Does one need to be baptized in the spirit to be saved?" Is no.

However, if one were to ask whether or not the Holy Spirit is necessary to live the way Christ intended; the answer is a resounding yes. As already discussed in the walking in the Spirit section, the Holy Spirit helps us exude Christ in our lives by teaching us what He expects from us. When we exude Christ, and hold fast to His teaching we will have a sense of peace and understanding as to our mission and purpose on Earth.

*"But the Helper, the Holy Spirit, whom the Father will send in My name, He will teach you all things, and bring to your remembrance all things that I said to you." John 14:26*

# Think About It

In the society we live in today, one could argue the Church is being persecuted as heavily as it was during its formation nearly 2,000 years ago. Of course the way in which this is happening is much different today. Those who oppose Christianity, look to censor the teaching and remove it from the public eye. Rather than kill the people associated with the teaching, as the early Church opposition did. Although in some parts of the world, Christians are still martyred in great numbers. The only way to continue Christ's work and push back against this persecution is through the help of the Holy Spirit. The battle we are fighting is waged completely in the spiritual realm and we aren't equipped to fight it on our own.

*"Finally, my brethren, be strong in the Lord and in the power of His might. Put on the whole armor of God, that you may be able to stand against the wiles of the devil. For we do not wrestle against flesh and blood, but against principalities, against powers, against the rulers of the darkness of this age, against spiritual hosts of wickedness in the heavenly places. Therefore take up the whole armor of God, that you may be able to withstand in the evil day, and having done all, to stand." Ephesians 6:10-13*

Why then do so many in the Church seek to discredit and ignore the Holy Spirit? Some even go as far as teaching that the Holy Spirit is really from Satan, which by the way is the only unpardonable sin.

*"Assuredly, I say to you, all sins will be forgiven the sons of men, and whatever blasphemies they may utter; but he who blasphemes against the Holy Spirit never has forgiveness, but is subject to eternal condemnation"—because they said, "He has an unclean spirit." Mark 3:28-30*

The Church must reengage with the Holy Spirit in order to remain relevant and avoid being silenced by the forces who oppose it. Don't listen to the words of men that tell you the Holy Spirit isn't for you or for the modern Church. Satan is smart; He will use false teachers such as these to weaken the Church. Check the scripture for yourself and see what the Word of God says. If you're a believer that has not been baptized in the Holy Spirit, don't hesitate another day to ask the Lord for this baptism.

# Chapter 4:
# The Hypocrite Church

Anyone that attends church regularly, or even semi-regularly, has most likely heard a sermon about how the world is getting worse quicker than ever before. A sermon like this is usually followed by using the empty seats of the church as an object lesson. "It's a lack of desire for Christ, that's why these seats are empty." Well, that's not necessarily true. It just happens to be easier to pass the blame to the "unchurched", than it is to examine why people have stopped attending. Regardless, it stirs applause in those attending on that particular Sunday. Maybe in your church the pastor doesn't preach on it, but the dwindling congregation size is definitely discussed in private. "Maybe people are getting bored with this pastor and we should get a new one." Stop it folks, please just stop.

These types of things are going on in churches all across the country, and the observation of the condition of humanity is correct. Of course the world is getting worse quicker than ever before. However, the reason so many people aren't in church is not because the world is so bad, the world is getting so bad because people aren't in church. Anytime people disconnect from God things decline rapidly. It is important to note the entire body of Christ is always referred to as the Church with a capital "C". If the "c" is not capitalized, the reference is to a physical building or place of gathering.

# What's the Problem?

So what then is the cause of fewer people showing up every Sunday in most churches? It seems few know what the problem is and those that do don't want to accept it. Forgive me for being the one to lay this truth on you Church, but the problem is you! I say this not to be unkind, but to hopefully open the eyes of the Church to be effective again. When the Church ceases to be effective, God will cut it off.

*"You will say then, "Branches were broken off that I might be grafted in." Well said. Because of unbelief they were broken off, and you stand by faith. Do not be haughty, but fear. For if God did not spare the natural branches, He may not spare you either. Therefore consider the goodness and severity of God: on those who fell, severity; but toward you, goodness, if you continue in His goodness. Otherwise you also will be cut off." Romans 11:19-22*

The natural branches in this passage are the Jews, God's chosen people. The ones grafted in are the gentiles, otherwise known as Christ's Church. The Jewish people were cutoff due to their unbelief and unwillingness to follow Christ. So here the apostle Paul is warning the Church that if they do not do the work Christ has called them to do, how much more likely are we to be cutoff. It only makes sense, that if the natural branches weren't sparred, why would the unnatural branches be?

# The Proof

Many of you reading this right now are having a really hard time accepting this. Some of you may even be angry that a person, let alone a minister, would say these things. The truth is I had a hard time accepting it myself when God laid this on my heart. But once a person gets past their own ego, they can really look around at the nonsense going on in the Church. They can also listen and analyze what those outside the Church are saying.

The biggest reason those who do not attend church give for not wanting to come is hypocrisy. According to a study done by LifeWay research, 72% of those who do not attend church said "the church is full of hypocrites."[3] Some of you are already trying to discredit that in your mind. "They are just bitter and anti-God; they don't know what they are talking about" you say. Actually, it turns out that from the same poll, 72% of respondents said they believe in God, 71% said Jesus makes a positive difference on one's life, and 78% said they would be willing to listen to a person share their Christian beliefs.

If the majority of respondents weren't anti-God, what was their reasoning for saying the church is full of hypocrites? Could it be that the Church is actually full of hypocrites? That would certainly explain why people say that it is. It would also explain why the Church is performing so lackluster. We all have a basic understanding of what a hypocrite is, someone who says one thing but does another. Let's look at how the Bible describes a hypocrite though.

*"Hypocrites! Well did Isaiah prophesy about you, saying: 'These people draw near to Me with their mouth, and honor Me with their lips, But their heart is far from Me. And in vain they worship Me, Teaching as doctrines the commandments of men." Matthew 15:7-9*

*"They profess to know God, but in works they deny Him, being abominable, disobedient, and disqualified for every good work." Titus 1:16*

There are many other examples, but I'm confident you get the point. From scripture we see that an individual, who claims to believe in God or to be a Christian, must carry out the will of the Lord through their actions. If they do not, they are considered a hypocrite.

So back to the original question, are the unchurched people correct about the Church being full of hypocrites? Turns out they are. Of course you can't just ask a person if they are a hypocrite or not, obviously any Christian would say no. So Barna Group put Christians to the test, to see if their actions matched up with their Christian words. The results are shocking. Out of the entire study, only 14% displayed Christ like actions and attitude![4] And the Church wonders why things have gotten as bad as they have. Fourteen percent with Christ like behavior is why!

To make matters even worse for the reputation of the Church, if that's possible, 50% of respondents in the same study displayed self righteous actions and attitude. The complete opposite of what Christ taught! Maybe that's why the definition of Christian changed from "one who exudes Christ like behavior" to "a religion based on the teachings of Jesus." Christianity is not a religion; it is a relationship with Christ. At least that's what it's supposed to be.

## What If We Don't Change?

The scripture tells us that the door to the gentiles, which is the Church, will eventually be closed once its purpose has been fulfilled. We looked at this earlier in the chapter pertaining to the branches being grafted in. At that time God will restore the chosen people of Israel and the focus will swing back to them. This does not mean that the Church can be lax because it will eventually be cut off anyway. Just the opposite, we must diligently keep the standards Christ set in place for Him to continue to extend grace to our country. One must understand that while the Church is one body under Christ, it has many members.

*"For as the body is one and has many members, but all the members of that one body, being many, are one body, so also is Christ." 1 Corinthians 12:12*

For instance, this means if the Church of the United States were to cease to follow what Christ set forth, but the Church of Canada continued walking in His statutes; He could remove His power and grace from the U.S, while the Church of Canada continued to thrive. And any nation, that God removes His grace from, will suffer miserably. The book of Revelation shows us how the Lord will deal with the Church who fails to do what He has commanded.

*"I know your works, that you are neither cold nor hot. I could wish you were cold or hot. So then, because you are lukewarm, and neither cold nor hot, I will vomit you out of My mouth. Because you say, 'I am rich, have become wealthy, and have need of nothing'—and do not know that you are wretched, miserable, poor, blind, and naked." Revelation 3:15-17*

It's not too late though folks, all that has to be done is return to His will for the Church and He will sustain us through the end.

*"As many as I love, I rebuke and chasten. Therefore be zealous and repent. Behold, I stand at the door and knock. If anyone hears My voice and opens the door, I will come in to him and dine with him, and he with Me." Revelation 3:19-20*

## Think About It

The current state of the Church in the U.S is one of self righteousness. It has become more of an exclusive club where people come to gather in their cliques. Rather than a place to come as you are and have your needs met by Christ. People have noticed this and walked away; leading to the closure of over 4,000 churches per year. Of course this is not the case of every church in the United States; there is still a remnant of the Church as Christ intended it. But for the most part, when it comes to the issues facing this modern world, the Church is hiding in the corner.

*"Who say, 'Keep to yourself, Do not come near me, For I am holier than you!"Isaiah 65:5*

This is not written to attack anyone, hurt feelings, or defame the Church. It is written out of love for Christ and the desire to see the Church thrive and reach the lost; albeit a tough love. But sometimes tough love is necessary, as any parent knows.

*"Furthermore, we have had human fathers who corrected us, and we paid them respect. Shall we not much more readily be in subjection to the Father of spirits and live? For they indeed for a few days chastened us as seemed best to them, but He for our profit, that we may be partakers of His holiness. Now no chastening seems to be joyful for the present, but painful; nevertheless, afterward it yields the peaceable fruit of righteousness to those who have been trained by it." Hebrews 12:9-11*

The Church can make a comeback. But it is up to each individual to display Christ through their actions. While writing this book I came across a social media post that read "Any Holy Ghost filled pastors going out to protest?"; referring to a racial protest taking place in a major U.S city. That is not how Christ operates, nor will He bless those types of actions from His Church. Anyone that is truly filled with the Holy Spirit knows that chaos doesn't bring about unity. Any Christian that participates in an event in which someone is breaking the law is guilty by association and brings about shame on the Church body. It is hypocritical and does not represent Christ.

However, when the Church collectively exudes Christ in their daily walk; by welcoming outsiders in without judgment, loving unconditionally, and forgiving as Christ forgave you, it will draw people to the Lord. Those outside the church will want what you have, feel comfortable coming to you, and you will see the empty seats begin to fill once more. A new pastor can't do it, fresh paint can't do it, and a coffee shop in the lobby can't do it. Can the Church stop the fighting between denominations, worrying about board meetings, and gossiping about one another; and just get back to praise, worship, and winning souls? That is totally up to you.

# Chapter 5:
# Making My Own Way

What a day in age we are living in, more technology than ever before and major scientific advancements like the world has never seen. If taken at face value, it seems like a great thing. Sadly, this increase in knowledge could be the very thing that causes people to turn away from God. In this age of information and advanced learning, the attitude of being self-made is more rampant than ever before. The more human beings learn, the more they believe that they are in control. This leads many to throw God to the side, believing Him to be nothing more than old superstition for the uneducated to follow. The word of God responds to this notion.

*"Professing to be wise, they became fools."*
*Romans 1:22*

Now don't get me wrong, I'm not against technology, modern conveniences, or advanced learning. In fact, I enjoy it as much as anyone else. But with the rapid increase in knowledge, comes the sign of the end times when Jesus will return, the Bible clearly states it. This of course is not a concern for those who are saved, having accepted Jesus Christ as their savior. For the unsaved though, this is crunch time.

*"But you, Daniel, shut up the words, and seal the book until the time of the end; many shall run to and fro, and knowledge shall increase." Daniel 12:4*

When the end will actually come, only the Lord knows. But it is our responsibility to know and understand the signs that will precede His coming.

*"Then He said to them, "Nation will rise against nation, and kingdom against kingdom. And there will be great earthquakes in various places, and famines and pestilences; and there will be fearful sights and great signs from heaven." Luke 21:10-11*

*"And there will be signs in the sun, in the moon, and in the stars; and on the earth distress of nations, with perplexity, the sea and the waves roaring; men's hearts failing them from fear and the expectation of those things which are coming on the earth, for the powers of the heavens will be shaken." Luke 21:25-26*

## Unbelievers

Despite the increase in knowledge this generation has been given, that does not give an individual the ability to make their own way. Nor has anyone ever had the ability to make their own way. Excuse the directness of this statement, but the "self-made man" mentality is as ridiculous of a thought as one could have. Man, and by that I refer to the human race, can barely walk and chew gum at the same time. Yet we think we can orchestrate a successful career, marriage, raise our kids, and have our dream house without the help of God? Good luck with all that. Without Him there wouldn't be one good thing in your life.

*"Do not be deceived, my beloved brethren. Every good gift and every perfect gift is from above, and comes down from the Father of lights, with whom there is no variation or shadow of turning." James 1:16-17*

If you don't believe that and don't believe in God then what is the harm in saying "Lord, if you're real then take everything I own away from me." Of course I'm being facetious, no one is to temp God. But a person that is atheist would be better off to do this and come to the realization of the Lord's existence and repent, than to keep their possessions and lose their soul.

*"For what will it profit a man if he gains the whole world, and loses his own soul? Or what will a man give in exchange for his soul?" Mark 8:36-37*

This is purposely harsh to get your attention. Every breath you breathe is given by God. You are not your own, Christ paid the price for you at Calvary that you might be saved. Don't be fooled by the knowledge of this generation, quit struggling to make your own way and let God take over. You won't be disappointed!

*"Trust in the LORD with all your heart, and lean not on your own understanding; in all your ways acknowledge Him, And He shall direct your paths. Do not be wise in your own eyes; Fear the LORD and depart from evil. It will be health to your flesh, and strength to your bones." Proverbs 3:5-8*

# Godless and Prospering

In the "wisdom" of the human mind, we try and reason out our surroundings. This becomes an issue as it pertains to understanding the provision of God. As already discussed in the chapter, we know all good things come from God. Then how does my neighbor, that doesn't serve God a lick, receive blessing after blessing? This defies Christian logic and can eventually lead one to begin to doubt God. Especially when difficulties come to the house of the faithful, and from our perspective, always skip over the house of the unfaithful. In the Christian mind, we feel as though since we are serving God we should be more blessed in this life than those who do not. Of course this is not the case.

*"But I say to you, love your enemies, bless those who curse you, do good to those who hate you, and pray for those who spitefully use you and persecute you, that you may be sons of your Father in heaven; for <u>He makes His sun rise on the evil and on the good, and sends rain on the just and on the unjust.</u>" Matthew 5:44-45*

Really take a look at the underlined part of the verse above. While it may not seem fair or make sense to us, God's plan is perfect. As a saved Christian, it really doesn't matter how many earthly possessions we have, because we already have eternal life and the knowledge of Christ. This does not mean we won't long for certain things. Rather that we can't get so caught up in our desire for possessions that we forget what we have in the Lord.

It is also important to remember that simply having possessions does not make one blessed. And the absence of trouble in your "blessed neighbors" life does not mean God is favoring them. Quite often, it is just the opposite. You see God may allow a person to obtain possessions and amass wealth to test them down the road to see which they will choose, Him or the possessions.

*"Then Jesus said to His disciples, "Assuredly, I say to you that it is hard for a rich man to enter the kingdom of heaven. And again I say to you, it is easier for a camel to go through the eye of a needle than for a rich man to enter the kingdom of God." Matthew 19:23-24*

Many people get comfortable in their earthly riches and it becomes like a prison cell, with the door wide open. God calls out for them to leave the riches of Earth to obtain riches in Heaven, but the allure of their comfy cell is too great to give up. Then one day, the cell door closes and all the stuff withers away and at that point it is too late to call out to the Lord. Of course the day of the door closing, is the day one breathes their last breath. In these cases it was actually the lack of trials in their life, that lead to the person's demise. So rejoice in your Christian trials, it more than likely means you're doing something right and Satan wants to stop it.

*"My brethren, count it all joy when you fall into various trials, knowing that the testing of your faith produces patience. But let patience have its perfect work, that you may be perfect and complete, lacking nothing." James 1:2-4*

# Believers

It's a shame that a believer even needs to be addressed when discussing the "self-made" mentality. Anyone who claims to be a Christian ought to know better than to believe they are the maker of their own destiny. Now don't read this the wrong way, in no way am I saying that a Christian lacks free will; because we absolutely do. What I'm trying to convey to you is that God's plan should be first and foremost on the mind of every believer. The reason being, His plan is perfect and we should pray and seek to fulfill that plan over ours.

*"For I know the thoughts that I think toward you, says the LORD, thoughts of peace and not of evil, to give you a future and a hope." Jeremiah 29:11*

Instead of seeking after the will of the Lord, many Christians dive into any opportunity that comes along and seems good. I'll be the first one to admit; I've been there and done it, several times. What a mess those situations turned out to be. Goes to show how slow of learners we human beings can be. But it's so hard when you have been praying and seeking God's will and no answer seems to be coming. A person has to do something though right? Can't just sit around and wait forever. Actually, waiting and being still before the Lord is exactly what we are supposed to do.

*"Rest in the LORD, and wait patiently for Him…" Psalm 37:7*

*"But those who wait on the LORD*
*Shall renew their strength;*
*They shall mount up with wings like eagles,*
*They shall run and not be weary,*
*They shall walk and not faint." Isaiah 40:31*

I know those scriptures most likely aren't new to those of you that have been walking the Christian path for years. But how many people that quote those verses about waiting on the Lord, also try and make their own way with the following explanation. "I'm waiting on the Lord, but while I'm waiting I'm going to (insert plan here). After all, God helps those who help themselves." WRONG, WRONG, and WRONG again!

Not to be unkind, but not only is that not Biblical; it's the opposite of the Word of God. Moses in Exodus chapter two is the perfect example of helping himself and trying to make his own way. Without being told to by the Lord, he killed an Egyptian slave master. As a result he spent forty years in the wilderness. Stay out of the wilderness Christians and quit trying to make your own way. This is what the word of God actually says about man trying to make his own way.

*"He who trusts in his own heart is a fool."*
*Proverbs 28:26*

For future reference the ridiculous notion that God helps those who help themselves was originally penned by Algernon Sydney in the mid 1600's. However, the quote was more famously reprinted by Benjamin

Franklin in the *Poor Richard's Almanac* in the mid 1700's.

## Think About It

If God's intention was for man to make his own way, why did he send Christ to pay for our sins? One could say that's all the help we needed, everything else we can blaze our own trail. With that logic, we should be able to blaze a trail directly to Christ. We're strong, smart creatures; surely we can figure it out. Then why did God appoint the fivefold ministry?

*"And He Himself gave some to be apostles, some prophets, some evangelists, and some pastors and teachers, for the equipping of the saints for the work of ministry, for the edifying of the body of Christ." Ephesians 4:11-12*

Clearly, not only did we need Christ to help reconcile us to God, but we also needed appointed teachers to get us to Christ. Outside of that though, we've got daily life figured out right? Wrong again. The Holy Spirit has to guide us daily to keep us from making critical errors; He even has to help us pray.

*"Likewise the Spirit also helps in our weaknesses. For we do not know what we should pray for as we ought, but the Spirit Himself makes intercession for us with groanings which cannot be uttered." Romans 8:26*

Millions of human beings hold the belief that they can get things done on their own. But almost all cry out to

God or whatever "higher power" they are acquainted with when life brings them to their knees. So why can't we just admit that we don't have all the answers and need help? The answer is pride, so deep rooted within us, the only way it can be extracted is to ask Christ into your heart. Don't waste any more time in your life trying to figure things out on your own, and only calling on God when you're in trouble. Form a relationship with Him now and let him guide you in His perfect plan; a plan which is greater than we could ever think.

*"For My thoughts are not your thoughts,*
*Nor are your ways My ways," says the LORD.*
*"For as the heavens are higher than the earth,*
*So are My ways higher than your ways,*
*And My thoughts than your thoughts." Isaiah 55:8-9*

# Notes

# Chapter 6:
# Multiple Roads

The belief that there are multiple roads that lead to Heaven isn't new. As is obvious, each different religion around the world has its own idea of how to get to Heaven or paradise. That is a whole book within itself, so I'll not get into the error of that. What I am referring to is the belief within Christianity itself that there are multiple roads to Heaven. A study done by Pew Forum showed that 57% of evangelical church goers believe in multiple ways to Heaven.[5] Has the Church lost its mind?!

*"Thomas said to Him, "Lord, we do not know where You are going, and how can we know the way?"Jesus said to him,* **"I am the way, the truth, and the life. No one comes to the Father except through Me."** *John 14:5-6*

The evidence of only one way into Heaven is evident throughout the Bible. In the scripture above, Jesus Himself tells us there is only one way, and that is through Him. So unless the Central American Church has entered the twilight zone, there must be some explanation for this lunacy, I mean it's written plain as day for all to see. Maybe a good portion of people can't read and therefore don't know what the Bible says. Farfetched but that would explain it! According to the U.S department of education, 86% of U.S citizens can read, sad that the percentage isn't higher; but that's of little concern compared to the topic at hand.[6] So if the vast majority of the population can read, then as suspected, reading is not the problem. Or is it?

## The Word of God, Again

As it turns out reading is the problem, not the lack of ability, rather the drive to do it. According to a LifeWay Research poll, only 20% of Americans have read the entire Bible.[7] Therein lays the problem. It is an impossibility to apply scripture to your life if you haven't studied it to begin with. Sure, many that don't read the Bible attend church services, but there are several issues with this approach to understanding the Word of God.

Relying on a church service to acquaint you with the Word of God is an inefficient and dangerous way to learn. Often times only a few scriptures are used as the basis for a sermon, and some sermons aren't based in scripture at all. This leads many sitting in the congregation that haven't read the Bible to wonder what is pastoral opinion and what is directly from the Word of God. As was stated in chapter three regarding discernment, without knowing the Word through your own study, a pastor can easily lead you down one of the multiple roads we are addressing in this chapter; and you would be none the wiser. Putting your soul on the line expecting another person to teach you is not wise, the Holy Spirit is the teacher and will reveal God's Word to you if you'll pick it up and read it.

*"These things I have written to you concerning those who try to deceive you. But the anointing which you have received from Him abides in you, and you do not need that anyone teach you; but as the same anointing teaches you concerning all things, and is true, and is not a lie, and just as it has taught you, you will abide in Him." 1 John 2:26-27*

Even if the pastor of your church is preaching Biblical sermons presented with scripture, it's a very inefficient way to learn scripture. With only 52 sermons a year, you'll never cover the entirety of the Bible. The job of a pastor is to lead and guide the church and expand on what you have already studied yourself. Think of it like a class in school, when the teacher told the class to read a certain chapter or book for discussion the next day, you knew you better do it or risk looking foolish. If you didn't read, when the teacher called on you, you had no earthly idea what was going on or what she was talking about.

Some of you are thinking I have strayed way off topic here. Aren't we supposed to be talking about multiple roads to Heaven? Well, we are. The theme above and beyond all else is getting back to the Word of God. My commentary is simply to direct you there and help you understand how far we've strayed from it. So I will continue to impress the importance of getting into the Bible for yourself throughout this book. The key to understanding every false doctrine is to understand the Bible. Now that we've went over all that again, we can progress.

# All Go to Heaven

Amongst Christians there are three major false beliefs of how to get to Heaven outside of Jesus Christ; all go to Heaven, good people go to Heaven, and those who do good works go to Heaven. I heard it said recently from a lovely elderly woman that "We're all headed to Heaven." Nice thought, but it couldn't be further from the truth.

*"Enter by the narrow gate; for wide is the gate and broad is the way that leads to destruction, and there are many who go in by it. Because narrow is the gate and difficult is the way which leads to life, and there are few who find it." Matthew 7:13-14*

The narrow gate and difficult way of course is Jesus Christ and living according to the principles set forth by Him. The difficulty in doing so is not due to the complexity of Christ's teachings or in asking Him to be your Savior, but rather the overwhelming pull of the sin nature in our life. The wide gate and broad way to destruction is the literal highway to Hell.

*"Again, the kingdom of heaven is like a dragnet that was cast into the sea and gathered some of every kind, which, when it was full, they drew to shore; and they sat down and gathered the good into vessels, but threw the bad away. So it will be at the end of the age. The angels will come forth, separate the wicked from among the just, and cast them into the furnace of fire. There will be wailing and gnashing of teeth." Matthew 13:47-50*

As is clear in the scriptures above there will be a separation from the saved and the unsaved. The choice of where you spend eternity however is yours, God will not turn away any who call upon the name of Jesus.

*"And this is the will of Him who sent Me, that everyone who sees the Son and believes in Him may have everlasting life; and I will raise him up at the last day." John 6:40*

Don't believe the lie that everyone will make it to Heaven. Heed the words of the rich man in scripture that mistreated the poor beggar named Lazarus.

*"Then he [the rich man] said, 'I beg you therefore, father, that you would send him [Lazarus] to my father's house, for I have five brothers, that he may testify to them, lest they also come to this place of torment." Luke 16:27-28*

# Good Guy Road

There is an overwhelming belief throughout the population that being a good person will get you into Heaven. The problem is there's no such thing as a good person in God's eyes, without the blood of Jesus.

*"There is none righteous, no, not one." Romans 3:10*

*"For all have sinned and fall short of the glory of God." Romans 3:23*

This is difficult for us as human beings, even Christians, to cope with when someone close to us dies. To think of the person we loved that meant so much to us, being in Hell is too much for many to bear. We convince ourselves, for the sake of alleviating our own pain, that they were a good person and surely God will accept them into Heaven. Unfortunately that is just not the case.

I say all this with a very heavy heart, knowing so many have been lost to this way of thinking. But I hold out hope for those still here, it's not too late to accept Jesus. If you or someone you know is terminally ill or if you witness an accident in which someone is mortally wounded, beg and plead with them to make Jesus their Savior before they pass. I beg and plead with you to accept Jesus into your heart right now. Because once a person draws their final breath, there's no changing the outcome; no purgatory and no second chances.

## The Road of Works

The most widely practiced and believed lie about making it to Heaven is that doing good works will get you there. It's easy to understand how a person may get that impression. Scripture has been misconstrued over the years by proponents of works based salvation.

*"Knowing that whatever good anyone does, he will receive the same from the Lord, whether he is a slave or free." Ephesians 6:8*

This particular scripture is not referring to earning something from God, as an employee earns pay from an employer. It is simply stating that the Lord will bless your life in return for the good you do to others. Not because He is obligated to, but because of His love for us, He gives willingly. In no way does this scripture or any like it refer to earning salvation.

Doing good works makes the flesh feel good though. We feel that when we do something for the Lord it gives us a little bit of control of our destiny. Almost like making payments on a car. The more you pay, the closer it gets to becoming yours. The more good works you do, the closer your salvation and the greater the reward in Heaven. That's a major fallacy and is completely opposite of all that Christianity stands for. Rituals and works won't save you, being good to others is just expected of any follower of Christ. The Bible makes it very clear on where works stand when it comes to salvation.

*"For by grace you have been saved through faith, and that not of yourselves; it is the gift of God, not of works, lest anyone should boast. For we are His workmanship, created in Christ Jesus for good works, which God prepared beforehand that we should walk in them." Ephesians 2:8-10*

*"Knowing that a man is not justified by the works of the law but by faith in Jesus Christ, even we have believed in Christ Jesus, that we might be justified by faith in Christ and not by the works of the law; for by the works of the law no flesh shall be justified." Galatians 2:16*

# Think About It

Accepting Jesus Christ as Lord and Savior is no more difficult than praying a simple prayer. But yet so many try and earn their way to Heaven, spending their entire lives working away trying to ensure salvation and constantly wondering if they've done enough. There are others that do nothing, believing they're good enough on their own to make Heaven. Both beliefs are inexcusable to the Lord. One cannot plead ignorance on the day of reckoning, stating that they didn't know better. The Word of God has made salvation clear; don't miss out on the splendor of God because of foolish pride.

*"Therefore submit to God. Resist the devil and he will flee from you. Draw near to God and He will draw near to you. Cleanse your hands, you sinners; and purify your hearts, you double-minded. Lament and mourn and weep! Let your laughter be turned to mourning and your joy to gloom. Humble yourselves in the sight of the Lord, and He will lift you up."*
*James 4:7-10*

# Chapter 7:
# We'll All Make Heaven

In the previous chapter we briefly touched on the belief that some have, that everyone will make it to Heaven. That belief is one that is spawned from a simple lack of knowledge. This chapter however will address the doctrine of Universal reconciliation or Universalism. This is a doctrine which states that a loving God would not send His children to Hell and therefore there is no Hell. Also, despite what anyone does in their life, they will ultimately be reconciled to God due to His mercy.

While some false doctrine can be attributed to man's misinterpretation, the doctrine of Universalism is straight from Satan himself. The greatest lie the Devil can get the world to believe is that there is no Hell and that God loves you too much to punish you for anything. Most think that Satan would not mention God to those He's trying to deceive, and ignore Him all together. That's not the case; Satan unfortunately is very wise and uses deceit mixed with a portion of the truth to confuse the children of God. He looks for those in ministry that are weak; to be the mouth that spews His lies.

*"For such are false apostles, deceitful workers, transforming themselves into apostles of Christ. And no wonder! For Satan himself transforms himself into an angel of light." 2 Corinthians 11:13-14*

*"So the great dragon was cast out, that serpent of old, called the Devil and Satan, who <u>deceives the whole world</u>; he was cast to the earth, and his angels were cast out with him." Revelation 12:9*

# Founded

While the proponents of Universalism claim it began at the formation of the Church as foundational doctrine, we know from scripture that could not be farther from the truth.

*"Then Peter said to them, "Repent, and let every one of you be baptized in the name of Jesus Christ for the remission of sins; and you shall receive the gift of the Holy Spirit." Acts 2:38*

If the foundational doctrine of the early Church held this belief, there would have been no need to tell anyone to repent. Eventually you would be forced to accept Jesus as your savior anyway, according to the Universalist belief. So the question of when exactly the belief began can't quite be pinpointed and answered with certainty.

Modern Universalism in the U.S can be pinpointed however to John Murray. Murray was originally a preacher of Calvinism in Ireland, which is a false doctrine itself that will be addressed in the next chapter. He left Ireland to visit London, where he was introduced to the Universalist movement being led by a man named James Relly. After reading publications from Relly and listening to him preach, Murray became a follower of the Universalist movement. On a side note, this is why it is so important for you as a believer to be firmly rooted in the true word of God and baptized in the Holy Spirit. Otherwise, one can easily be deceived by a smooth talking false teacher.

Soon after converting to Universalism, many of Murray's family died and he had a falling out with the rest. This is what led him to make the decision of heading to America. Bound for New York, the ship Murray was on had some issues and he ended up in New Jersey. There he preached his first Universalist sermon on American soil; the date was September 30, 1770. Murray eventually settled in Massachusetts and served as the pastor of the first Universalist church in America. In 1790 he helped to officially form Universalism as a denomination. John Murray died in 1815 and is still known today as the father of American Universalism.[8]

# Universalism Foundational Scripture

In this section the scriptures that the Universalists use as their foundational doctrine will be laid out. Read through the scriptures and notice how the proponents of this doctrine have simply cherry picked through the Bible to support their viewpoint. The underlined words are the catch words they use to ensnare people in their false belief.

### Universal Restoration
*"Whom heaven must receive until the times of restoration of all things, which God has spoken by the*

*mouth of all His holy prophets since the world began."*
*Acts 3:21*

### No Separation
*"And by Him to <u>reconcile all things to Himself</u>, by Him, whether things on earth or things in heaven, having made peace through the blood of His cross."*
*Colossians 1:20*

### Ultimate Salvation
*"That at the name of Jesus <u>every knee should bow</u>, of those in heaven, and of those on earth, and of those under the earth, and that every tongue should confess that Jesus Christ is Lord, to the glory of God the Father." Philippians 2:10-11*

### Cleansing Through Purgatory Fires
*"But who can endure the day of His coming? And who can stand when He appears? For <u>He is like a refiner's fire</u>, and like launderers' soap." Malachi 3:2*

# Fallacy of Universalist Scripture

Now let's go through each of these foundational scriptures of Universalism and debunk them with the entirety of the Word of God. The bold text is the scripture you read in the previous section and underlined portions will now be the words that debunk the false belief of this doctrine.

### Restoration
There is a restoration that will take place on Earth and to God's people. This restoration does not mean that all

people will be restored to a position with God. When the scripture is read in context, this becomes clear.

*"<u>Repent</u> therefore and <u>be converted, that your sins may be blotted out</u>, so that times of refreshing may come from the presence of the Lord, and that He may send Jesus Christ, who was preached to you before,* **whom heaven must receive until the times of restoration of all things, which God has spoken by the mouth of all His holy prophets since the world began.** *For Moses truly said to the fathers, 'The L<small>ORD</small> your God will raise up for you a Prophet like me from your brethren. Him you shall hear in all things, whatever He says to you. And it shall be that <u>every soul who will not hear</u> that Prophet <u>shall be utterly destroyed</u> from among the people." Acts 3:19-23*

## Separation

Universalists teach there is no permanent separation from God or ultimate destruction; the end state of a person is in a blessed reunion with the Father. Sounds great, but in reality every promise of God is conditional and a believer must do their part not to fall away.

**"And by Him to reconcile all things to Himself, by Him, whether things on earth or things in heaven, having made peace through the blood of His cross....<u>if indeed you continue in the faith</u>, grounded and steadfast, and <u>are not moved away</u> from the hope of the gospel which you heard, which was preached to every creature under heaven, of which I, Paul, became a minister."**
*Colossians 1:20,23*

*"In flaming fire taking vengeance on those who do not know God, and on those who do not obey the gospel of our Lord Jesus Christ. These shall be punished with everlasting destruction from the presence of the Lord and from the glory of His power."*
*2 Thessalonians 1:8-9*

### Salvation

In Universalist doctrine, they present ultimate salvation. This means, according to their belief, that God is powerful and loving enough to cause all souls to be saved. If God's power causes all to be saved, then free will to chose whether to serve Him or not goes out the window.

*"And if it seems evil to you to serve the LORD, choose for yourselves this day whom you will serve."*
*Joshua 24:15*

The scripture Philippians 2:10-11 as basis for the doctrine that everyone will confess Jesus is based on truth, but the Universalists take it out of context. Yes, everyone will eventually confess Jesus as Lord; some as savior, but others as a judge.

**"That at the name of Jesus every knee should bow, of those in heaven, and of those on earth, and of those under the earth, and that every tongue should confess that Jesus Christ is Lord, to the glory of God the Father."** *Philippians 2:10-11*

*"For we must all appear before the judgment seat of Christ, that each one may receive the things done in the*

*body, according to what he has done, whether good or bad." 2 Corinthians 5:10*

The words of Jesus Himself completely debunk the teaching that He will eventually save everyone, including those who rejected Him. Of course it is God's desire that all be saved through His Son, but God leaves the decision to us.

*"For as the Father has life in Himself, so He has granted the Son to have life in Himself, and has given Him authority to <u>execute judgment</u> also, because He is the Son of Man. Do not marvel at this; for the hour is coming in which all who are in the graves will hear His voice and come forth—<u>those who have done good, to the resurrection of life</u>, and <u>those who have done evil, to the resurrection of condemnation</u>." John 5:26-29*

### Purgatory Fires

So according to Universalists, is it God that is forcing you to come back to him or is it Jesus eventually saving you from separation? They say there's no Hell though, so what are you being saved from? They don't even quite know what they believe, but they sure think you're crazy if you don't follow them. In all this confusion, they've thrown in purgatory which is borrowed from Catholicism, for those who don't receive salvation while on Earth. The Universalists purgatory, or waiting place for God, supposedly has cleansing "fires" or trials to remove negative human attributes. This gives the person the opportunity for conversion.

*"But who can endure the day of His coming?
And who can stand when He appears? For He is like
a refiner's fire, and like launderers' soap."*
*Malachi 3:2*

What the scripture is saying here is that Christ will come to cleanse one of their sins and inequities; if they accept Him. It is not talking about a place of purification if we don't get it right during our time on Earth. There are only two places to go when you die, into eternal Hell or eternal Heaven. That is why scripture presses the importance of accepting Christ quickly.

*"And these will go away into everlasting punishment, but the righteous into eternal life." Matthew 25:46*

*"For He says: 'In an acceptable time I have heard you, And in the day of salvation I have helped you.' Behold, now is the accepted time; behold, now is the day of salvation." 2 Corinthians 6:2*

# Think About It

The entire Bible from the Old Testament through the New Testament speaks of a Savior. Jesus Christ, whom man must accept in order to have eternal life or be eternally lost. There is no in between and God is not going to force you to serve Him or be in His presence.

The Universal reconciliation movement can be tricky to spot or seem somewhat accurate on the surface. Proponents will mention God, Jesus, and the Holy

Spirit. They will also tell you they believe in the Bible. The problem is Universalists take parts of scripture and attempt to make doctrine out of it. Their teaching is flimsy at best and damning at worst. It is a teaching that makes people feel warm and fuzzy in their lackadaisical behavior.

Many authors and filmmakers are getting in on the theme and producing fictional works based on the idea of Universal reconciliation. Now that you have the background on it, know how to recognize it, and have scripture to refute it; there is no reason for you to fall prey to it. If you know friends or family members that hold this belief, do your best to reach them with the truth before it's too late.

# Notes

# Chapter 8:
# Once Saved, Always Saved

In a wide variety of denominations, there are many people that believe that once a person has received their salvation from the Lord; they can never lose it. Unfortunately, that is not the case. I once heard a great man of God say, "Getting people saved is easy, keeping them saved is hard." The same man would then joke, that immediately after a person got saved, it would be better for them to get knocked in the head with a club and go to be with the Lord then continue living and back away from God. While of course no one is advocating that, the thought does illustrate a valid point.

Accepting Christ is easy, and many do. Life after receiving salvation though, has a way of dragging a person down with tests, trials, and temptation from Satan. This tends to lead many back away from God, losing their salvation in a backslidden state. A person cannot lose their salvation by not doing enough good works or not following a certain formula for living, it can only be lost by turning back to the world and away from God. Note that once a person backslides, they can return to the Lord and repent. Some teach that once you fall away once that's it, don't believe that! As long as you're still breathing and in your right mind, the Lord will accept you back if you ask.

# The Belief Begins

Once saved, always saved is a belief that in part came from a doctrine known as Calvinism. I say "in part" because this is not the main teaching of Calvinists. Imagine the game telephone, where you stand in a line and the first person whispers a phrase to the next person in line and so on until the phrase reaches the last person. The last person in line will without a doubt say a different phrase due to human error. This is exactly how once saved, always saved came from Calvinism; even though that belief is not entirely accurate to what the Calvinists teach.

# Calvinism

Now that you have an idea of how this belief came from Calvinism, we'll look at the entire doctrine that they teach. Not only will studying Calvinism help you to understand why once saved, always saved is not scriptural; it will help you avoid becoming a victim of the falsities of this sect.

Calvinism as you may have guessed is named for its founder, John Calvin. Calvin was a European who lived from 1509-1564 and was originally known as a scholar rather than a preacher. His role as a preacher however, began once he had fled from France to Switzerland due to the discord between himself and the Roman Catholic Church.[9] Calvin's teachings are referred to in the acronym TULIP, which we will briefly cover.

## Total Inability

Calvin taught that all human beings are completely consumed by sin, every ounce of a person. This part is Biblically accurate (Jeremiah 17:9), meaning there is nothing good in man that he can earn salvation. Had Calvin stopped there he would have been alright. After all it is correct that there is no good in man without Christ, and salvation can definitely not be earned.

But, he took things a step further. Calvin proposed that due to sin, man is helpless and completely unable to understand the Gospel. Along with not being able to understand the Gospel, man does not have the ability to come to Christ unless God overpowers that person and gives him the ability to do so.

## Unconditional Election

This part of Calvin's doctrine comes from a clear misinterpretation of scripture in the Apostle Paul's letter to the Roman's.

*"For whom He foreknew, He also predestined to be conformed to the image of His Son, that He might be the firstborn among many brethren. Moreover whom He predestined, these He also called; whom He called, these He also justified; and whom He justified, these He also glorified." Romans 8:29-30*

Calvin took this way out of context, and stated that predestination meant that God had already chosen who to save and who He was going to send to Hell. That is in no way accurate. What God predestined was His plan of salvation, not the planned destination of each individual's soul. Calvin taught that one could only hope they are predestined for Heaven, but that they had no choice in the matter whether they were or not.

## Limited Atonement

This belief held by Calvinist's is quite simple; Jesus didn't die for all. Calvin taught that the death and atonement of Jesus Christ was only for those we just discussed, those that are predestined to be saved. As for everyone else, Jesus didn't die for you according to Calvin. How he came to this way of thinking is anyone's guess. The thought that Jesus only died for a few contradicts so many scriptures, it's hard to see how one could even draw that conclusion.

## Irresistible Grace

Again, this Calvinistic stance is simple. God predestined some to be saved, Jesus died for those whom He predestined, and now through "irresistible grace" forces those He predestined to be saved. Calvin states that for those selected by God, you have absolutely no choice but to accept salvation. Proponents attempt to say that the reason that this grace is irresistible is due to the Holy Spirit pulling and forcing us to submit to it. As has been covered numerous times throughout this book, the Holy Spirit doesn't force us to do anything.

## Perseverance of the Saints

This is it; the once saved, always saved doctrine of Calvinism. Calvin believed and taught that once a person was saved, they were eternally secure in that salvation and could never walk away from it. Of course, the only people that can be saved according to Calvin are those that are already chosen, so what does this have to do with those who are not Calvinists? Well, this is where the telephone game comes into play. What started out as something like, **"All those who are predestined by God to receive salvation, shall never lose it."**; then became, **"Those who receive salvation from God shall never lose it."** Through the years, after being passed along over and over again it eventually became **"Once saved, always saved."** A good way to miss Heaven is to believe once you are saved you can do whatever you want and still make it. Please don't make that mistake.

# Refuting Calvinism

It doesn't take much searching of the scripture to refute Calvinism. Here are a few of the many which prove it false.

### Total Inability
*"The mystery which has been hidden from ages and from generations, but now <u>has been revealed</u> to His saints." Colossians 1:26*

There is no mystery inside the Word of God, all has been revealed in a way all can understand. The saints referred to in this scripture are not a small preselected group, but rather anyone who looks on the Lord and believes.

*"But <u>you are not willing</u> to come to Me that you may have life." John 5:40*

*"I have come in My Father's name, and <u>you do not receive Me</u>; if another comes in his own name, him you will receive." John 5:43*

Notice the wording Jesus uses. He says **"you are not willing"** and **"you do not receive."** The Lord was very methodical in every word that He spoke, not once did He ever misspeak. So if it were accurate that man does not have the ability to come to Him, He would have said "you cannot come" and "you cannot receive." The wording here makes human choice very clear.

### Unconditional Election

*"For this is good and acceptable in the sight of God our Savior, who <u>desires all men to be saved</u> and to come to the knowledge of the truth." 1 Timothy 2:4*

Clearly if God's desire is for all men to be saved, He is not going to only select a few to be eligible for salvation.

*"The Lord is not slack concerning His <u>promise</u>, as some count slackness, but is longsuffering toward us, <u>not willing that any should perish</u> but that <u>all</u> should come to repentance." 2 Peter 3:9*

God never breaks a promise, and His promise was salvation through Jesus Christ made available to the entire world. As we see in the scripture here, He is not willing that any perish; meaning go to Hell. This completely refutes the Calvinistic teaching that God destines some to Heaven and some to Hell.

*"He who believes in the Son has everlasting life; and he who does not believe the Son shall not see life, but the wrath of God abides on him." John 3:36*

Again, here we see a clear choice given to us through free will. Choose to accept Jesus or don't, God's not going to force you. But if you don't accept Him, there will be consequences.

## Limited Atonement

*"And He [Christ] Himself is the propitiation for our sins, and not for ours only but also for the whole world." 1 John 2:2*

*"And He [Christ] died for all, that those who live should live no longer for themselves, but for Him who died for them and rose again." 2 Corinthians 5:15*

As is obvious, Christ died for all, not just a select few. This does not mean that a person is covered by the sacrifice Jesus made without formally accepting Him. The door to acceptance is open and available to everyone if they so choose.

## Irresistible Grace

*"Because I have called and you refused,
I have stretched out my hand and no one regarded."
Proverbs 1:24*

Once again, accept God or refuse Him. It's your choice and He won't force you.

*"You stiff-necked and uncircumcised in heart and ears! You always resist the Holy Spirit; as your fathers did, so do you." Acts 7:51*

As we have already discussed, the Holy Spirit leads you, He doesn't force you. Despite the fact that Calvinists may say the opposite, we see in this verse that human beings can and do resist the Holy Spirit.

### Perseverance of the Saints

*"My people are bent on backsliding from Me. Though they call to the Most High, None at all exalt Him." Hosea 11:7*

*"Brethren, if anyone among you wanders from the truth, and someone turns him back, let him know that he who turns a sinner from the error of his way will save a soul from death and cover a multitude of sins." James 5:19-20*

As the scripture has shown, there are no predestined people to be saved. Therefore, Calvin's teaching that those predestined to be saved cannot lose their salvation, makes no sense. However, the once saved, always saved crowd is still out there.

If one studies the scripture above, they will clearly see the intent of man. People are bent on turning away from God, and the result of that turning away is wandering from the truth. When one wanders from the truth, the result is death. The truth that this verse is speaking of is salvation. Bring that all together and you have the ability of a human being to walk away from their salvation which will result in that person missing out on Heaven.

## Think About It

The once saved, always saved belief that one cannot lose their salvation, is one of freedom. It comforts a person and has a freeing effect for them to know that once they accept Jesus, they are good forever. It gives a sense of security, knowing they can let their guard down and slip back into the ways of the world. Churches that teach this often have large congregations, due to the warm fuzzy feeling the members get when they hear from the pulpit that they are eternally secure; cozier than a cup of hot chocolate next to a crackling winter fire.

It's just too bad the whole line of teaching is a sham. A pastor that loves their congregation should long to tell them the truth. Their concern should not be about congregation size or how popular they are. As we have seen scripturally there is no Biblical evidence that supports once saved, always saved theology. And given that a pastor should know scripture better than anyone, there should be no reason for this false teaching. If you have heard this from someone other than a pastor, I trust that you did your due diligence and looked to the scripture yourself to see whether it is accurate or not. As a person should with any teaching they hear.

If you're reading this book, I can't help but believe you are an intelligent person. Using that intelligence ponder this; if you pick something up, can you not put it down?

Sure you can; just as you can accept salvation through Jesus Christ or walk away from Jesus Christ and your salvation. If you pick up a snake and it bites you, would you not let it go? Of course you would, most of you wouldn't grab a snake to begin with. Don't hold on to the belief that once you're saved, you're always saved, no matter your actions. That doctrine is a snake, don't pick it up. If you do, it will eventually bite you.

# Chapter 9:
# Grace! Let's Party!

Grace is God's free unmerited favor or assistance given to humans for regeneration or sanctification. This is the foundation of the New Covenant which came through Jesus Christ, which of course is the greatest thing to ever happen to mankind. However, some in the modern Church have managed to spin God's grace into a false doctrine; known as the Grace Movement. Some may wonder, "How can the basis for the entire New Covenant be spun into false doctrine?"

## Grace Movement

The answer is excess; "hypergrace" if you will. Grace is a wonderful thing; we owe our entire lives to God's grace. But as with anything else in the world, it can be overdone. Water is great for keeping your body healthy and functioning properly. However, too much water ingested too fast will kill you. Think about your favorite plate of food, now imagine you go to put a sprinkle of salt on it and the lid falls off the salt shaker. Your plate of food is now ruined by something that was originally intended to make it better.

This is what is happening within the grace movement. Grace is being portrayed by many as a right to live however you want after receiving Christ as savior. Unfortunately, as we've seen in previous false doctrine addressed within this book, people flock to this kind of teaching. Hypergrace is often indirectly and discreetly taught as a license to sin without repentance; while maintaining your salvation. The reason for this discreetness is to avoid being called out by those who are firmly rooted in God's word.

Imagine a grace movement leader coming out on stage and proclaiming, "You can do whatever you want as long as you're saved!" Anyone with any Biblical knowledge at all would know that is not correct and would leave that ministry. So these hypergrace preachers slide the ability to sin and get away with it carefully into their sermons. They'll often use sweet and elegant speech to woo their audience. This way, people focus more on *how* the minister is speaking, rather than *what* they are speaking. When confronted with the issue of why abstaining from sin is not taught; many of these pastors simply respond "grace." What does the word of God say?

*"What shall we say then? Shall we continue in sin that grace may abound? Certainly not! How shall we who died to sin live any longer in it?" Romans 6:1-2*

Those two verses alone sink the hypergrace boat. By not condemning unrepentant sin, those who teach this hypergrace theology may very well condemn your soul. What exactly is considered sin though and how does a new believer know if their church addresses it or not?

# Original Sin and Law

There are two types of sin that one must understand. The first is known as original sin, which one is born into. The second type of sin is an action carried out by a person against the will of God.

## Original Sin

This is the condition of every human being ever born, with the exception of Christ. Through the fall of Adam and Eve in the Garden of Eden, sin entered the world.

*"Therefore, just as through one man sin entered the world, and death through sin, and thus death spread to all men, because all sinned— (For until the law sin was in the world, but sin is not imputed when there is no law." Romans 5:12-13*

Original sin could not and cannot be atoned for by anything but the blood of Jesus Christ.

## Sin in Action

The act of sin is controlled completely by an individual. It is not a condition passed from one generation to the next. While the existence of sinful actions were around long before Moses, God gave him the Ten Commandments to help guide the morality of humanity; namely the Israelites at the time. This is known as the Law of Moses, the basis for the Old Covenant. The Ten Commandments are the basic outline for avoiding sin. They are as follows.

1. You shall have no other Gods before me.
2. You shall not make for yourself a carved image (idol).
3. You shall not take the name of the Lord in vain.
4. Remember the Sabbath day to keep it Holy.
5. Honor your father and your mother.
6. You shall not murder.
7. You shall not commit adultery.
8. You shall not steal.
9. You shall not bear false witness against your neighbor.
10. You shall not covet.

**Exodus - Ch. 20**

While the law outlined God's basic morals, it had no power to overcome sin. Nor could man keep the law due to the pull of original sin within them. This is why you see mankind longing for a redeemer in the scripture of the Old Testament. In God's grace He sent His Son Jesus to be that Savior.

*"For what the law could not do in that it was weak through the flesh, God did by sending His own Son in the likeness of sinful flesh, on account of sin: He condemned sin in the flesh, that the righteous requirement of the law might be fulfilled in us who do not walk according to the flesh but according to the Spirit." Romans 8:3-4*

# Grace in Christ

As previously stated, in God's amazing grace, He sent His Son to pay the price for the sins of mankind that we may be reconciled to God. Through Christ one can now be saved by grace through faith rather than live and die by the works of the law, this is the New Covenant.

*"For by grace you have been saved through faith, and that not of yourselves; it is the gift of God, not of works, lest anyone should boast." Ephesians 2:8-9*

If you remember that scripture from earlier in the book, good job! These two verses are essential to understanding the New Testament and New Covenant. Sadly, the hypergrace crowd has misconstrued the meaning of the grace mentioned here. They along with others say that God's grace through Christ eliminates us from needing to keep the Ten Commandments; stating that Christ eliminated the Law of Moses. That is incorrect; Christ did not eliminate the law, He fulfilled the Law.

*"Do not think that I came to destroy the Law or the Prophets. I did not come to destroy but to fulfill. For assuredly, I say to you, till heaven and earth pass away, one jot or one tittle will by no means pass from the law till all is fulfilled. Whoever therefore breaks one of the least of these commandments, and teaches men so, shall be called least in the kingdom of heaven; but whoever does and teaches them, he shall be called great in the kingdom of heaven. For I say to you, that unless your righteousness exceeds the righteousness of the scribes and Pharisees, you will by no means enter the kingdom of heaven." Matthew 5:17-20*

As we see here, Christ didn't eliminate the law and free us from keeping it. He actually told us to keep the Law with His own words. Jesus then went on to expound on the Law and outline what sin under the new covenant looks like.

# New Covenant Sin

The proponents of the grace movement teach the freedom from sin, and the need to repent; due to grace in Christ. When in actuality, Christ detailed sin even more clearly than the Ten Commandments did and raised the bar of expectation rather than lower or remove it; why though? This is because the Lord knew that when one accepts Him, they have power to overcome sin.

*"For sin shall not have dominion over you, for you are not under law but under grace." Romans 6:14*

This power over sin comes to a believer when they accept Christ and He cleanses them from original sin. Free from original sin through Christ's sacrifice, the person also receives power from the Holy Spirit. Thus Christ raised the bar, knowing His children would have the ability to keep those instructions through the help of the Holy Spirit, should they choose to.

Despite the ability to overcome sin, one will never reach perfection in the flesh. This is partially due to our lack of engagement with the Holy Spirit. As human beings we often roam about doing what feels good, rather than what is right. Regardless, the following outlines what Christ expects of us and defines as sin.

*"You have heard that it was said to those of old, 'You shall not murder, and whoever murders will be in danger of the judgment.' But I say to you that whoever*

*is angry with his brother without a cause shall be in danger of the judgment. Matthew 5:21-22*

*"You have heard that it was said to those of old, 'You shall not commit adultery.' But I say to you that whoever looks at a woman to lust for her has already committed adultery with her in his heart." Matthew 5:27-28*

*"Furthermore it has been said, 'Whoever divorces his wife, let him give her a certificate of divorce.' But I say to you that whoever divorces his wife for any reason except sexual immorality causes her to commit adultery; and whoever marries a woman who is divorced commits adultery." Matthew 5:31-32*

*"You have heard that it was said, 'An eye for an eye and a tooth for a tooth.' But I tell you not to resist an evil person. But whoever slaps you on your right cheek, turn the other to him also." Matthew 5:38-39*

*"You have heard that it was said, 'You shall love your neighbor and hate your enemy.' But I say to you, love your enemies, bless those who curse you, do good to those who hate you, and pray for those who spitefully use you and persecute you." Matthew 5:43-44*

You can see in these verses how the Law was expanded on. Now we will look at the teaching of Christ above and beyond the Law. As you read through what Christ considers sin and teaches us to abstain from, understand that He doesn't ask us to do these things as a dictator. The Lord isn't set out to ruin your fun here on Earth, but His mission is for us to be ambassadors for Him and further the kingdom of God. Thus, we need to follow His instructions and abstain from these things to be an effective witness for Him.

*"Now the works of the flesh are evident, which are: adultery, fornication, uncleanness, lewdness, idolatry, sorcery, hatred, contentions, jealousies, outbursts of wrath, selfish ambitions, dissensions, heresies, envy, murders, drunkenness, revelries, and the like; of which I tell you beforehand, just as I also told you in time past, that those who practice such things will not inherit the kingdom of God." Galatians 5:19-21*

*"But now you yourselves are to put off all these: anger, wrath, malice, blasphemy, filthy language out of your mouth." Colossians 3:8*

*"Do you not know that you are the temple of God and that the Spirit of God dwells in you? If anyone defiles the temple of God, God will destroy him. For the temple of God is holy, which temple you are."
1 Corinthians 3:16-17*

*"Do you not know that the unrighteous will not inherit the kingdom of God? Do not be deceived. Neither fornicators, nor idolaters, nor adulterers, nor homosexuals, nor sodomites, nor thieves, nor covetous, nor drunkards, nor revilers, nor extortioners will inherit the kingdom of God." 1 Corinthians 6:9-10*

*"And even as they did not like to retain God in their knowledge, God gave them over to a debased mind, to*

*do those things which are not fitting; being filled with all unrighteousness, sexual immorality, wickedness, covetousness, maliciousness; full of envy, murder, strife, deceit, evil-mindedness; they are whisperers, backbiters, haters of God, violent, proud, boasters, inventors of evil things, disobedient to parents, undiscerning, untrustworthy, unloving, unforgiving, unmerciful; who, knowing the righteous judgment of God, that those who practice such things are deserving of death, not only do the same but also approve of those who practice them." Romans 1:28-32*

## Think About It

The instructions that Christ gave us in order to live a righteous life are expected to be kept. When we mess up, which we will, we must still ask for forgiveness despite the fact we are under grace. Many want to argue and try to justify their sinful behavior by saying "The Bible doesn't say I can't do (such and such)." Sure there are some things in modern day culture that are not mentioned specifically in the Bible. That is why God gave us the ability to reason out other scripture such as these to discern right from wrong.

*"But beware lest somehow this liberty of yours become a stumbling block to those who are weak."*
*1 Corinthians 8:9*

This scripture in 1 Corinthians makes it clear that we are to avoid doing anything that would cause another person to sin or fall away. Even if what we are doing is not listed as a sin in the Bible. This next scripture follows along that same line.

*"Abstain from every form of evil."*
*1 Thessalonians 5:22*

Some translations of this verse use the term "appearance" instead of "form". To abstain from even the appearance of evil, makes any doubt about certain behavior clear. Even if what you're doing is completely innocent, it should be avoided at all costs if it appears evil to an onlooker.

For instance, if people know you are a married Christian; it wouldn't be a great idea to go to dinner alone with someone of the opposite sex who is not your spouse. Not because you are doing anything wrong, but because it may start a rumor that can affect your Christian witness. Remember, the world flocks to drama, and false statements travel much faster than the truth.

If you truly love God, keep His commandments. Do what He asks you to do out of respect for all that He's done for you. Will having a drink of alcohol or smoking a cigarette send you to Hell? Of course not, but ask yourself if that's the best you have to give God. Are you doing all you can to further the Kingdom?

Don't let the grace doctrine fool you, if you do wrong you must ask the Lord for forgiveness. Sure He is gracious to forgive you over and over again, but think of how you feel when the same person repeatedly wrongs you, but then asks forgiveness. It gets old real quick doesn't it? Praise God that He is long suffering, but don't take advantage of it. Do your part to live as you should.

# Notes

# Chapter 10:
# Lord Make Me Rich!

I bet you didn't know that Christ came into the world, not only to atone for sin, but to make you filthy rich as well! Don't believe it? Then read for yourself, it says it right here in the Bible.

*"The thief does not come except to steal, and to kill, and to destroy. I have come that they may have life, and that they may have it more abundantly." John 10:10*

See there, Jesus said that He wants us to have an abundant life. That obviously means that He wants to give us a nice big house, a new car, and the best promotions at work! Not buying it? Does it seem a bit off to you? Good, because it's absolute nonsense. Yet tens of thousands are buying into this prosperity Gospel and "name it and claim it" ministries. Easy enough to understand why, they are teaching things we all want to hear. Our human nature wants to be comfortable. We want to be blessed with abundance to live the life we always dreamed. Never mind little to none of that teaching is Biblical.

## The Abundant Life

Some of you might be offended right now because you enjoy listening to prosperity preaching. Rather than take offense though, understand that those who love you will tell you the truth even if it's not popular. They will not just tell you what you want to hear in order to line their own pockets. Other people may be thinking that if the prosperity Gospel isn't accurate, they are destined to be poor. That's not the case either. As human beings we tend to swing from one extreme to the other. Some even teach one must be in a poverty state to truly serve the Lord. That belief is false as well.

The real mindset of a Christian should not be on the state of your personal finances anyhow. Sure we have to pay the bills, but that is secondary to the state of our relationship with Christ. Think of the old quote from JFK, "Ask not what your country can do for you, but what you can do for your country." That should be our way of thinking, pertaining to our relationship with Christ. Don't seek Him for what He can do for you; seek Him for who He is.

*"But seek first the kingdom of God and His righteousness, and all these things shall be added to you." Matthew 6:33*

So what is abundant life outside of money and possessions? We have an abundant life simply by accepting Christ. In that we are freed from the bondage of sin and operate in the gifts of the spirit to further the Kingdom. The Lord's abundance is a mindset and state of being, a feeling of self worth knowing who you are in Christ and that He created you for a purpose. No amount of wealth can replace a feeling of inadequacy or lack of one's sense of purpose.

A person must understand that while abundance in the Lord doesn't mean Earthly wealth, one can still be blessed financially. That plan however is up to the Lord, no formula, no words, and no works are going to cause God to make you rich. If the Lord were to make all who follow Him rich, many would fall away into worldly distractions and follow their own desires rather than His.

*"It is easier for a camel to go through the eye of a needle than for a rich man to enter the kingdom of God." Mark 10:25*

# Prosperity Gospel

The entirety of the prosperity Gospel hinges on just a few key verses, some of which we will cover in this section. Many of these verses are taken out of context. Other verses are only partially stated, yet presented in a way that makes it seem like that's exactly what the scripture says and means. Within prosperity teaching, two fundamental beliefs exist; the first being that Christ intended us to be rich through His sacrifice.

### Rich in Christ
*"For you know the grace of our Lord Jesus Christ, that though He was rich, yet for your sakes He became poor, that you through His poverty might become rich." 2 Corinthians 8:9*

If one glosses over this scripture and reads it superficially, they might believe that Christ actually died to make us wealthy. That is completely out of context. Break the scripture down and really study it. The Lord was rich in Heaven, and then He came to Earth. Here He lived as we do, minus the engagement of sin, and grew up in a poor household. In those days there was no middle class, you were either rich or poor. As a carpenters "son" He was definitely not considered rich. By living on Earth in this way, He was able to pay the price for our salvation through His perfect sacrifice. With that sacrifice we become rich with access to eternal life, not possessions.

## Prosperity Formula

The second way prosperity preachers teach that one can attain riches is by giving. Now that in itself has a Biblical backbone in the form of tithing.

*"Will a man rob God? Yet you have robbed Me!*
*But you say, 'In what way have we robbed You?'*
*In tithes and offerings. You are cursed with a curse,*
*For you have robbed Me, Even this whole nation.*
*Bring all the tithes into the storehouse, That there may*
*be food in My house, And try Me now in this,"*
*Says the LORD of hosts, "If I will not open for you the*
*windows of heaven and pour out for you such blessing*
*that there will not be room enough to receive it."*
*Malachi 3:8-10*

The principle of tithing is not that we give in order to receive a blessing. We are to give because everything that we have is due to God's favor. As discussed in chapter five, none of us make our own way.

The blessings mentioned in this scripture are not necessarily reimbursed and increased finances. While the Lord may very well bless us financially for giving to His work, there is no set formula as to what you may receive back. Nor should you expect there to be. Those blessings could be your car not breaking down or the furnace not going out, thus saving you a lot of money. Again, there is no set formula and no timeline as to when you will see these blessings. Give with a joyful heart, without expecting to get something immediately in return and you will be blessed.

*"But this I say: He who sows sparingly will also reap sparingly, and he who sows bountifully will also reap bountifully. So let each one give as he purposes in his heart, not grudgingly or of necessity; for God loves a cheerful giver. And God is able to make all grace abound toward you, that you, always having all sufficiency in all things, may have an abundance for every good work." 2 Corinthians 9:6-8*

Giving should never be taught in any way beyond the principle of tithing, or with the expressed idea that you will be directly financially blessed. If you are listening to someone that is teaching this, run away, turn the television off, whatever it takes to get away from that fallacy. The following scriptures can help to indentify these prosperity ministries; especially if they are used over and over as the basis for a sermon.

*"And we know that all things work together for good to those who love God." Romans 8:28*

That scripture will often rally a round of applause. In hard times, it's great to hear that everything is going to turn out for the best. But wait, isn't there more to that scripture?

*"And we know that all things work together for good to those who love God, <u>to those who are the called according to His purpose</u>." Romans 8:28*

There it is; the part of the verse that puts a condition on that promise. All things only work together for good if you're doing God's will and carrying out His purpose. If a person spends their Saturday nights drinking alcohol and proceeds to get in a fight or get in a drunk driving accident, don't think that is part of God's plan for good. The misinterpretation of this verse actually has many convinced that they can do whatever they want and God will use it for good. No, don't believe you can do your own thing, and that when bad circumstances arise it's just God working things out for good. Not to be unkind, but that's ridiculous.

*"<u>Give, and it will be given to you: good measure, pressed down, shaken together, and running over</u> will be put into your bosom. For with the same measure that you use, it will be measured back to you." Luke 6:38*

Typically, when prosperity preachers quote this scripture, they only quote the underlined portion. Coincidentally enough, it's usually before an offering is taken. The interesting thing is, in context, this scripture isn't referencing money at all. The verse is actually talking about judging others. The measure to which you judge someone, is how you will be judged; and even greater so. This scripture can be used for other attitudes and actions as well. Think of it in conjunction with sowing and reaping. While one could make a loose connection to financial blessings with this verse, it's best to leave it the way the Lord intended it.

*"Who shall not receive a hundredfold now in this time?" Mark 10:30*

Out of this partial verse in the book of Mark, prosperity preachers have created a formula for financial blessing. I should say rather, they think they've found a formula for financial increase. These preachers will actually state that if you give a certain amount of money, it will come back to you one hundred times greater. In that case, let's all go grab $1,000 and give to these ministers that figured out this magic formula. Then each of us that gave will have $100,000 to reinvest back into the ministry. Then in just a short while we'll receive our $1,000,000. Why aren't more people doing this? We can all be millionaires if we just follow this simple formula!

Stop, seriously, the madness has to stop. This verse is not referring to riches. In fact, it's only five verses prior in Mark 10:25 that Jesus just mentioned how hard it is for a rich man to enter Heaven. In context, the Lord is saying that those who give up earthly riches for His sake will receive abundantly in Heaven.

# Name It and Claim It

Slightly different from the prosperity Gospel movement is the word of faith movement. While they both advocate worldly possessions, the way in which they believe one receives them is a bit different. Word of faith teaches that we have the power in our words to "name it, and claim it." Literally meaning whatever we speak and ask for, we will receive. This again is a misinterpretation of scripture with an element of truth to it.

*"You lust and do not have. You murder and covet and cannot obtain. You fight and war. Yet you do not have because you do not ask." James 4:2*

The underlined portion of the above verse is all you will ever hear from a word of faith preacher. You have not, because you ask not. Some of you may have tried this and found that it doesn't quite work that way. Why not? Again, because of the conditions God puts on His promises. In the following verse of scripture, it answers why we can't and won't just have anything we proclaim that we want.

*"You ask and do not receive, because you ask amiss, that you may spend it on your pleasures." James 4:3*

Everything that we ask must be in accordance with God's will in order for us to receive it. So there is a small glimmer of truth to the teaching. But only in the way of asking according to His will.

*"And whatever you ask in My name, that I will do, that the Father may be glorified in the Son. If you ask anything in My name, I will do it." John 14:13-14*

Again, whatever we ask should be asked in order to glorify God. In asking for two new jet-skis and a hot tub, we don't bring Him glory. And no matter how many times you ask for it to appear, it's not going to happen. Now you may eventually get a jet-ski and hot tub, but I promise you it wasn't through a miracle that you received it. Is a bunch of stuff really what your relationship with God is about anyway? In ten years or so none of it will matter, forget about possessions and put your mind on Him.

## Think About It

There are people all over the world that barely have enough to eat and no sanitary water to drink. The United States along with many other countries have tens of thousands of homeless and poverty stricken people. Yet there is a whole group of so called Christians lining up to get into prosperity Gospel churches to hear how to receive their blessing. Focused solely on what God can do for them, rather than what they can do for others. And many Christians wonder why people aren't coming to church? That's because those outside the church see selfish people looking to further their own agenda in much of modern mainstream Christianity. That may not be the intent of the hearts of those attending prosperity churches, but it all goes back to perception as discussed in the previous chapter.

This self seeking garbage is NOT the true representation of the Church and what Christ intended it to be. But that is exactly what is often portrayed on social media platforms and television. Why is that? Because they have the biggest congregations, due to the prosperity teaching; thus giving them financial freedom to appear in mainstream media sources that smaller congregations cannot. Let's bring back the true Gospel of Jesus Christ and be the blessing, rather than continuously seek a blessing.

*"The generous soul will be made rich, and he who waters will also be watered himself." Proverbs 11:25*

*"For whoever gives you a cup of water to drink in My name, because you belong to Christ, assuredly, I say to you, he will by no means lose his reward." Mark 9:41*

# Chapter 11: God's a Jerk

The title of this chapter may seem harsh or offensive to a Christian. But unfortunately, God is called much worse than a jerk by many nonbelievers and ex-Christians alike. The idea that God hasn't done His part is a driving force behind unbelief. While most won't admit this openly due to a feeling of vulnerability, the fact still remains. When questioned intently about God, one who has walked away from Him or claims they don't believe will often give a nonchalant answer. For instance, "My views have just evolved" or "Rational thinking doesn't leave room for God."

However, if a person is persistent in questioning a nonbeliever or one who has left the faith, the majority of the time a deeper reason will come to light. For the person who has never believed, something may have happened in their childhood that made them think "If there is a God, that wouldn't have happened." For the ex-Christian, the most likely reasoning for abandoning God is an unanswered prayer or tragedy taking place. Whatever the reason may be, a person must come to the knowledge that God is always with us in the midst of the storm. Recently I heard this said by an ex-Christian, "God left me, He abandoned me." That could not be further from the truth.

*"Be strong and of good courage, do not fear nor be afraid of them; for the LORD your God, He is the One*

*who goes with you. He will not leave you nor forsake you." Deuteronomy 31:6*

## Feelings of Abandonment

To those who feel abandoned by God, ask yourself this question and answer honestly. Did God abandon you, or did you abandon Him? You see many times Christians get comfortable in their lifestyle, and cease to do their part to maintain their relationship with God. Often times we exchange the Bible for the remote control and Sunday morning church service for a day at the lake. Progressively we get farther away from God. Then when something in our life goes astray, we wonder where God was in the situation.

Why'd you leave me God? Why'd you pull back from me? God didn't back away, you did. Don't expect Him to chase you. A relationship is a mutual coming together. Meet God half way and do your part, and your feelings of abandonment will be no more. That doesn't mean God won't use silence for a season to increase your faith. Silence is just a reality of the growing process with God. It may be difficult for awhile, but keep doing your part; He is still right there with you.

*"Therefore humble yourselves under the mighty hand of God, that He may exalt you in due time, casting all your care upon Him, for He cares for you." 1 Peter 5:6-7*

# Unanswered Prayer

Unanswered prayers, more than a country song by Garth Brooks; are a reality of Christian life. One must understand that a prayer not being answered does not mean that God does not care about the situation. But rather that He has a plan to get you where He wants you to be. And that plan may be contrary to what you are praying for.

*"Now this is the confidence that we have in Him, that if we ask anything <u>according to His will</u>, He hears us. And if we know that He hears us, whatever we ask, we know that we have the petitions that we have asked of Him." 1 John 5:14-15*

Note the underlined portion of the scripture above. When we pray it must be according to the Lord's will for it to come to pass with positive outcome. For example, let's say a person is continuously praying for a promotion at work, but God's will is for that person to start their own business. Chances are that individual is so consumed by praying for that promotion, they can't hear what God is telling them to do. In order then, for God's will of them starting their own business to come to pass, they end up getting fired from the company where they so badly wanted a promotion.

This is when a person can become confused and maybe even angry with God. The time between the closed door and the one God is opening for us is crucial to us prospering in His will. If we choose to humble ourselves and listen to what He desires for us to do, success through His plan will come. On the contrary, if we get angry and attempt to go our own way, failure will ensue. Thus the process would begin all over. Leading us to deal with the disappointment and stress from a failed attempt at success yet again. If one refuses to listen to the Lord, this process can continue indefinitely until the opportunity to accomplish what God wanted them to do has passed, or death comes to them.

*"He who heeds the word wisely will find good, And whoever trusts in the LORD, happy is he."*
*Proverbs 16:20*

## Allowed to Fail

An often misunderstood principle of prayer is that it has the ability to bring about the wrong result if it's not rooted in God's will. That just blew some of your minds, but it's the truth. If we continuously pray for God to give us something, He may in fact grant our request and allow us to have what we so desire. Despite it being against His will. This does not apply to situations that could bring extreme harm, but to situations that can serve as a learning experience. These situations help us realize that we must trust and follow His plan, rather than ours, to be successful.

I'll use myself as an example. Years ago I desperately wanted to buy a cheap run down house and fix it up to sell for a profit. This is known as flipping. I had done a lot of studying on it, and knew other people doing it that were making a lot of money. In my mind I had already decided I was going to do it, with no regard for what the Lord wanted me to do. However, to do it I needed a partner. I prayed and prayed to find a partner; if I just had a partner I knew this would be the way to quick money. Finally, a partner came along and I started praying for a particular house I wanted. I would pray every night to get this house. Prayer answered, I got the house!

Up to this point I'm praising God for opening this door, despite the fact that I still hadn't ask Him if this is what He wanted. At the time, I was naïve enough to believe that God would not answer a prayer and open a door if it wasn't His will; I was wrong. What was planned to be a two month renovation and one month on the market to sell it; became a nine month renovation and two months on the market before it sold. Throughout the process there was one disappointment after another with the house renovation and within my life in general. What an absolute nightmare.

My wife and I later referred to this house as Hagar, Abrahams mistress that bore him a son outside of God's will. Because that's exactly what we did, we stepped out of His will and He answered those misguided prayers to teach us a lesson. Don't get so caught up in your own desires that you put God's will aside. You may just end up with a prayer you wish hadn't been answered and a Hagar of your own. And if you do, don't blame God for what sprung from your own error.

*"So I gave them over to their own stubborn heart,
To walk in their own counsels." Psalm 81:12*

# Tragedy Strikes

In every life, bad things happen. That is part of our journey here on Earth. To some, tragedy comes in unimaginable ways. Bringing with it pain, sorrow, and anger. We must understand though, that the presence of tragedy does not mean the absence of God. For a true Christian this can be very difficult to cope with. There is a false belief permeating through the Church, that if one is close enough to God and in His will, nothing bad will ever happen in their lives. That way of thinking will be devastating to a believer when something bad, unexpectedly happens. This can lead one to fall way from God.

*"These things I have spoken to you, that in Me you may have peace. In the world you will have tribulation; but be of good cheer, I have overcome the world."*
*John 16:33*

Jesus himself said that we would have tribulation in the world. Don't let any preachers or self help authors tell you otherwise. We know that at some point trials and tribulations will come, but that doesn't make them any easier to deal with when we are in the midst of them. Only Christ can ease our pain in a time of distress. Why do times of trouble have to come at all though? Scripture tells us.

*"Therefore, having been justified by faith, we have peace with God through our Lord Jesus Christ, through whom also we have access by faith into this grace in which we stand, and rejoice in hope of the glory of*

*God. And not only that, but we also glory in tribulations, knowing that tribulation produces perseverance; and perseverance, character; and character, hope. Now hope does not disappoint, because the love of God has been poured out in our hearts by the Holy Spirit who was given to us."*
*Romans 5:1-5*

Tragedy that comes according to God's will, always has a purpose behind it. For instance, to an unbelieving couple whose young child dies, this may be the time that they come to know the Lord. In this circumstance, the child under the age of accountability goes to Heaven. And both parents, who were unbelievers before, are now destined for Heaven as well. Granted they stay in the will of the Lord. Had the child lived a full life, the parents may have never come to know the Lord and the child may not have either. Though for a time here on earth, dealing with this type of tragedy is almost unbearable. The end result of salvation and eternal life far outweighs the temporary hurt during this lifetime.

*"For our light affliction, which is but for a moment, is working for us a far more exceeding and eternal weight of glory, while we do not look at the things which are seen, but at the things which are not seen. For the things which are seen are temporary, but the things which are not seen are eternal." 2 Corinthians 4:17-18*

One must also understand that many tragedies that come in life are not God's will. Acts of terrorism, rape, drunk driving deaths, and the like are not God's will.

God will however, comfort His children through His mercy in these times of tragedy, if one will allow. Do not get caught up trying to blame God for the evil acts of men's freewill; those thoughts only drive a wedge between you and God.

*For in the time of trouble He shall hide me in His pavilion; In the secret place of His tabernacle He shall hide me; He shall set me high upon a rock. Psalm 27:5*

## Adversity and the Unbeliever

If it wasn't so tragic to see people that refuse to accept God, it would almost be amusing to listen to them talk about how difficult life can be. Of course seeing someone struggling with life is not something to be scoffed at, as followers of Christ we should do all we can to help those in need. What is interesting though, is how so many people will try just about anything to make their lives better, but refuse to give God a try. The major reason for this is God has requirements, and He sets a standard for living that forces an individual to choose between His plan and their own.

Our plans will eventually lead to disappoint and failure at some point, while the Lord's will not. A person can read every self help book out there and not find peace without God. You can spend thousands of dollars on therapy and not find comfort without the Holy Spirit. And one can bury themselves in drugs and alcohol, seeking to forgot about their situation, but will never have deliverance without Jesus Christ.

Trying to navigate life without God is like trying to swim across the ocean with your hands and feet tied together while wearing a two hundred pound weight vest. It's going to be a constant struggle and eventually you will drown. A person may be able to skate through life on their own for awhile, but at some point in life, something will bring you to your knees; something bigger than any human being can handle. What do you do now? Christians turn to Christ for strength, support, and deliverance. Can another human being provide that?

Some would say yes; those are the ones who haven't experienced it yet. Sooner or later without a doubt, the people you think you can count on will let you down. In that place of extreme distress, without God, feeling alone and helpless, is where the thoughts of suicide creep in. Trials and tribulations come in life, but to those without God they can be life altering or ending. Don't wait until trouble comes, or until all other resources fail to seek God. Find Him now; learn to trust Him when things are going well, then you will be able to lean on Him when the trials come.

*"Trust in the LORD with all your heart, and lean not on your own understanding; In all your ways acknowledge Him, And He shall direct your paths. Do not be wise in your own eyes; Fear the LORD and depart from evil." Proverbs 3:5-7*

# Think About It

God tells us in His word time and again that He has our best interests at heart. He tells us that he cares about us and loves us. He wants to prosper our hand in His will and He will never leave us. Yet Christians and non-Christians alike blame God for their problems. They follow after their own lusts and desires, and then wonder why they fail and why God didn't help them out. Truth is He wants to, but we're often too stubborn to listen. Our failure is not God's fault; we choose through our actions what we will reap, not only in this life, but our eternal life as well.

*"But in accordance with your hardness and your impenitent heart you are treasuring up for yourself wrath in the day of wrath and revelation of the righteous judgment of God, who "will render to each one according to his deeds": eternal life to those who by patient continuance in doing good seek for glory, honor, and immortality; but to those who are self-seeking and do not obey the truth, but obey unrighteousness—indignation and wrath."*
*Romans 2:5-8*

One should always remember that with the presence of good, comes the presence of evil here on earth. Until the day Satan is thrown into the lake of fire, there will be negative circumstances here on earth. The Devil has power here to temp us, and through that temptation lead us to destruction. God is not a mean little kid burning ants with a magnifying glass, to think of Him that way is foolish.

Difficult circumstances that come in our life can be attributed to three sources; God, Satan, or ourselves. Difficulties that God allows will always produce a positive outcome and spiritual growth. Difficulties stemming from Satan or our own stupidity will not work out for our benefit. That is why it's so important to stay engaged with God, seek His will, and resist the Devil to live in a way that makes life worthwhile.

*"Do not be afraid of sudden terror, Nor of trouble from the wicked when it comes; for the LORD will be your confidence, and will keep your foot from being caught." Proverbs 3:25-26*

# Notes

# Chapter 12: Salvation Experience

To one who has not accepted Jesus Christ as their personal savior, describing the experience is nearly impossible. Words can't express the weight that is lifted off your shoulders. A sense of peace immediately falls over you, while simultaneously receiving power from the Holy Spirit who is now able to abide within you. The presence and knowledge of God becomes so real and so strong, that the most confident atheist could not deny it.

To those who have accepted Christ as your savior; are you living accordingly? If not, it's time to get it together. No more excuses, no more lackadaisical behavior; get to doing what Christ has asked you to do. None of us are perfect; we all have things we need to work on. Maybe there is something in this book that has ruffled your feathers or made you think twice about your church or your actions. The time to change it is now, the Church needs your full commitment to accomplish the great commission. Whatever you do for God, make sure it is His will. There are a lot of people doing "work for God" that isn't what the Lord has instructed. Not only does that not benefit the Church, it could end up costing you your soul.

*"Not everyone who says to Me, 'Lord, Lord,' shall enter the kingdom of heaven, but he who does the will of My Father in heaven. Many will say to Me in that*

*day, 'Lord, Lord, have we not prophesied in Your name, cast out demons in Your name, and done many wonders in Your name?' And then I will declare to them, 'I never knew you; depart from Me, you who practice lawlessness!" Matthew 7:21-23*

# Final Plea

As I hope you have seen throughout this book, the need for every human being to come to the knowledge and acceptance of Christ is paramount. The scriptures we have looked at, along with many others, make it very clear; Heaven and Hell are real places, and the only way into Heaven is through Jesus Christ.

*"And these will go away into everlasting punishment [Hell], but the righteous into eternal life [Heaven]." Matthew 25:46*

*"Thomas said to Him, 'Lord, we do not know where You are going, and how can we know the way?' Jesus said to him,* **'I am the way, the truth, and the life. No one comes to the Father except through Me.** *" John 14:5-6*

It doesn't matter how good of person you are, we all have sin in our lives as Romans 3:23 states. That is why, as shown in the scripture above, one must accept Christ to make it to Heaven.

*"For all have sinned and fall short of the glory of God." Romans 3:23*

My question to you, who refuse to accept or acknowledge the Lord, is a simple one. What do you have to lose by accepting Christ and living accordingly? Let's say hypothetically it's all a sham, and God isn't real. When you die the same thing will happen as if you hadn't accepted and lived for Christ anyway. The only difference would be the legacy you leave behind.

However, if God is real and you refuse to accept Christ; the outcome is eternal punishment and unimaginable torment in fires that will never be extinguished. Think back to the story of the rich man and Lazarus. The rich man begged for just a single drop of water on his tongue and remembered all the bad things he did in his life. The torment won't just be physical; it will be emotional as well. Imagine being in excruciating pain while at the same time having it brought to your remembrance over and over again why you are there; like a highlight reel of you at your worst in life. Thinking of all the chances you had to accept the Lord and refused, like this one right now as you read this book.

Many skeptics claim that it isn't rational to believe in God; when in fact, you've just been shown the opposite. If God is real and accepting Him has no negative consequences, but not accepting Him has eternal consequences; then to not accept the Lord is irrational! The only reason one truly doesn't want to accept Christ is because of the sin they would have to give up. Listen folks; the parties, the drugs, the alcohol, the fornication, or whatever your vice is, isn't worth refusing Christ over. The joy and pleasure one receives from knowing the Lord far exceeds what one gives up. In fact, once you accept Jesus Christ you won't even remember why you use to do the things that you did. Following Christ is not about what you have to give up, it's about what you have to gain and give others.

## Salvation Prayer

If you haven't accepted the Lord Jesus Christ, now is your chance. The Word of God shows us how easy it is.

*"That if you confess with your mouth the Lord Jesus and believe in your heart that God has raised Him from the dead, you will be saved. For with the heart one believes unto righteousness, and with the mouth confession is made unto salvation." Romans 10:9-10*

Simply reciting this prayer won't save you, but rather believing in your heart the words you're confessing will. Recite and believe the following prayer.

**Lord Jesus,**

**I believe in my heart you are the son of God; crucified on a cross, buried, and raised from the dead. I confess my sins and ask you to come into my heart. I make you my Lord and Savior. Amen!**

If you just prayed that prayer, congratulations! Welcome to the family. If you're not in church, I encourage you to find one that preaches the entirety of the Bible. Maintain a constant prayer life and seek God's will. Try and read your Bible daily to grow spiritually in the Lord. Follow these simple steps and your life will be fulfilling. God has amazing things in store for you!

# Personal Salvation Experience

# Afterword

I pray that you were blessed by this book. If all the information was something you already knew, praise God! I hope in that case it gave you the ability to explain these principles more easily to others. As I said in the beginning, the information within this book is not meant to attack or offend anyone. The purpose of it is to get the Church back on track, prevent those that are vulnerable from being swayed by false teaching, and Lord willing; convince unbelievers to accept Christ.

I'll admit parts of this book are harsh. But the Church has had plenty of wake up calls that it hasn't responded to. And sometimes tough love is the only thing that will get the job done. For instance, if a cow is down too long and won't get up, it will die. So the farmer will yell, pull on the tail, or smack the cow several times to try and get it up. The farmer doesn't do this to be mean; he does it to save the life of the cow. This book is the farmer, and the Church in America and many other countries is the cow. If the Church doesn't get up and start doing what it was intended to do; like the cow, it will die.

Some of you may be disappointed that I didn't attempt to prove God's existence throughout this book. I apologize if you feel that way. But the truth is, proving or disproving God's existence is not possible. Of course to those of us that have accepted Him and felt His power and love, there is no doubt He exists. To those who don't believe even after reading this book, answer a few questions for me. Did the clothes you are wearing just appear or did someone create them? If you put a stick of dynamite in the middle of a pile of building materials, will a finished house be the result of the explosion?

If you answered honestly, you said that someone created and made your clothes. You also said no to a house being built by an explosion of building materials. In fact, just the opposite; an explosion in a pile of building materials would create even more of a scattered mess than it was before. Therefore, if it's only rational to believe that there's a creator behind the creation of your clothes and a builder behind the construction of a house; then it's irrational to believe that we as humans came from evolution rather than creation. It's also irrational to believe that we live in a world formed by an explosion of material, rather than a builder assembling that material in an organized fashion.

I'm well aware that many public Christian figures and false teachers may rebuke this book. But realize that anyone who does is not rebuking my opinion, but the word of God itself. Those who do this, do so for personal gain, not your well being. You see many who teach the falsities exposed in this book, have a lot of money to lose if people catch on to the error of their ways. They may claim I'm jealous of their success.

When a person points out to someone they have food on their face, is it because they are jealous of them? Of course not, it's because they don't want them to look foolish. In as much, this book's purpose is to point out false teaching so people can walk away from it and not appear foolish.

Those who stand up for the truth are often persecuted; it's part of the Christian walk. This book portrays the truth, and I encourage you to tell others about it. If you liked the book give it a positive review online, if you didn't keep quiet and let others form their own opinion. I'm only joking, but seriously, don't hate on the truth!

God Bless!
Rev. Josh W. Jones

*"If the world hates you, you know that it hated Me before it hated you. If you were of the world, the world would love its own. Yet because you are not of the world, but I chose you out of the world, therefore the world hates you. Remember the word that I said to you, 'A servant is not greater than his master.' If they persecuted Me, they will also persecute you. If they kept My word, they will keep yours also. But all these things they will do to you for My name's sake, because they do not know Him who sent Me. If I had not come and spoken to them, they would have no sin, but now they have no excuse for their sin. He who hates Me hates My Father also. If I had not done among them the works which no one else did, they would have no sin; but now they have seen and also hated both Me and My Father. But this happened that the word might be fulfilled which is written in their law, 'They hated Me without a cause.'" John 15:18-25*

# Goals to Improve
# <u>My Walk with Christ</u>

# References

[1] Newport, Frank. (2016, June 29).
Most Americans Still Believe in God.
Retrieved from
http://news.gallup.com/poll/193271/americans-believe-god.aspx

[2] Saad, Lydia. (2017, May 15).
Record Few Americans Believe Bible Is The Literal Word Of God.
Retrieved from
http://news.gallup.com/poll/210704/record-few-americans-believe-bible-literal-word-god.aspx

[3] Jones, Sarah Bruyn. (2008, January 19).
72% say Church is Full of Hypocrites.
Retrieved from
http://www.tuscaloosanews.com/news/20080119/72-say-church-is-full-of-hypocrites

[4] Barna Group. (2013, June 3).
Christians: More Like Jesus or Pharisees?
Retrieved from
https://www.barna.com/research/christians-more-like-jesus-or-pharisees/

[5] Alcorn, Randy. (2008, July 23).
American Evangelicals Believe There Are Different Ways to Heaven.
Retrieved from
http://www.epm.org/blog/2008/Jul/23/american-evangelicals-believe-there-are-different-

[6] HuffPost. (2013, September 6).
The U.S. Illiteracy Rate Hasn't Changed in 10 Years.
Retrieved from
http://www.huffingtonpost.com/2013/09/06/illiteracy-rate_n_3880355.html

[7] Banks, Adelle M. (2017, April 25).
The Bible: Helpful But Not Read Much.
Retrieved from
https://religionnews.com/2017/04/25/the-bible-helpful-but-unread/

[8] French, Kimberly. (2009, June 29).
John Murray's Conversion to Universalism.
Retrieved from
http://www.uuworld.org/articles/john-murray-conversion

[9] Christianity Today. (n.d).
John Calvin: Father of the Reformed Faith.
Retrieved from
http://www.christianitytoday.com/history/people/theologians/john-calvin.html

Made in the USA
Lexington, KY
29 August 2018